# Get
# Of Our Own Way

## Love Is The Only Answer

# Michele Doucette, M.Ed.

Getting Out Of Our Own Way: Love Is The Only Answer

ISBN 978-1-935786-24-5

Printed in the United States of America by

St. Clair Publications

PO Box 726

McMinnville, TN    37111-0726

http://stan.stclair.net

# Table of Contents

Dedication ............................................................. 1

Author's Note ...................................................... 2

Reviews ................................................................ 4

Foreword ............................................................. 8

Fear ................................................................... 16

Conditioning ...................................................... 29

Anger ................................................................ 43

Inaction ............................................................. 50

Neutrality .......................................................... 56

Detachment versus Apathy ............................... 62

Knowledge versus Wisdom ............................... 74

Compassion and Compassionate Allowing ......... 81

Love is the New Religion ................................... 92

Selfishness versus Selflessness ......................... 99

Mindfulness ..................................................... 105

Integral Spiritual Practices ............................... 110

Discernment .................................................... 118

Indifference ..................................................... 123

Suppression versus Unboundedness.................................... 130

Transcendence ............................................................... 135

Antagonism.................................................................... 151

Empowerment ................................................................ 155

Positivity....................................................................... 164

Visionary Christianity .................................................... 171

Dharma ......................................................................... 182

Utopia ........................................................................... 185

Inspiration..................................................................... 187

Authenticity ................................................................... 191

Celebrating Diversity ...................................................... 199

Conscious Creation.......................................................... 205

The Ascension Finale ....................................................... 222

Sing a Song.................................................................... 234

Addendum ...................................................................... 237

Bibliography .................................................................. 247

About the Author............................................................ 280

# Dedication

Liam Matthew Boehner (May 29, 2011 to June 12, 2011), whose journey, albeit short, was incredibly meaningful. In keeping with synchronicity, this particular writing exists as published volume number twelve.

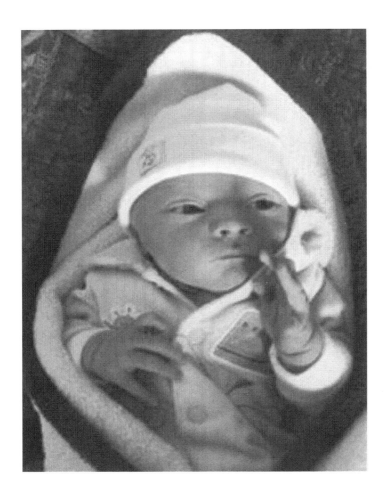

# Author's Note

In the course of my writing, there continue to be times when thoughts and words continue to simply present themselves. I have learned to both gracefully and thankfully accept that which comes to me in this fashion.

I AM Mind. I AM Consciousness. Everything that exists is a result of mental creation (thought, word, imagination), meaning that if I want to change something, I must first begin by changing my own mind.

The future that I encounter, therefore, depends on how I look at (feel, think, visualize) my world.

We attract to us, through the Law of Attraction, the very future that we anticipate.

It becomes in finding your heart, that you find your way.

It becomes in living the life you are meant to live, that you also find your way.

As Kevin Schoeninger so aptly puts it … *the meaning of life is the meaning you give to it.*

In the words of Sheryl Crow … *it is not about getting what you want, it is about wanting what you've got.*

Michele Doucette has done a wonderful and articulate job of assimilating and communicating the teachings that the Company of Light (celestials, galactic, and ascended masters) have provided us with in recent times, all of which are aimed at preparing us for a planetary shift, expected on, or before, December 21, 2012. It is very clear that she speaks from her own deep understanding and experience. I found reading this book to be both energizing and inspiring, and fully expect that her readers will experience the same.

Steve Beckow

The 2012 Scenario

http://stevebeckow.com

The Writings of Brother Anonymous

http://www.angelfire.com/space2/light11/index.html

Michele Doucette's love of research is matched by a joy and confidence that delivers one surprising turn after another as she leads you on a tour of your mind. On this tour, she serves up a stimulating and revealing exposé of what is required to get out of your own way.

Above all, this author inspires trust.

Put yourself in the hands of Michele Doucette and let her show you the way out of the prison of thoughts and conditioning.

Not only do I thoroughly enjoy the work she puts into her books, but I am deeply appreciative of how she presents the material.

Jerry Katz
Nonduality.com
Editor, One: Essential Writings on Nonduality

This book is a *must read* for all who are on the spiritual path. Unknowingly, we have all been programmed from a tender age (and sometimes even earlier). Continued through mass media, this programming greatly impacts how we live our lives. Understanding our "programs" becomes the first step towards true freedom and enlightenment. *Getting Out Of Our Own Way: Love Is The Only Answer* is a book that connects the dots beautifully; one that I highly recommend.

Jean-Guy Poirier

It is the instinctive need of every human being, whether realized or not, to achieve lasting peace of mind. Unfortunately, each is socially conditioned, and programmed with negative thinking, by the very society into which we are born.

In *Getting Out Of Our Own Way: Love Is The Only Answer,* Michele Doucette, as in none of her previous works, shows us how to identify the core issues and negative teachings

6

that keep us enslaved, thereby helping us to own our part in the problem.

In vivid parallel, she then helps us pinpoint simple steps to illuminate these negative teachings so that they may be replaced with positive energy, thus reclaiming the power which has always been ours.

Travel with Michele through this stimulating journey of the mind, and arrive in the ecstasy of freedom and spiritual empowerment. An extremely uplifting work, and one that I highly recommended, for those who have the desire to reach deliverance from negative social programming.

Stanley J. St. Clair, author of *Prayers of Prophets, Knights and Kings, Mysterious People of the Bible in the Light of History, On the Origins of the Clichés and Evolution of Idioms* and other books.

*Everything is comprised of energy. Everything is vibration. All vibration is the result of energy in motion. Energy is held together to create matter while matter is merely energy condensed to a slow vibration.*

*There is one underlying field of energy (the Zero Point Field) that pervades everything, thereby giving purpose and unity to our world.*

*Everything in the universe has a unique vibrational energy. Every object, every being, every thought, every action, every psychological mood; in short, energy equals vibration. Energy and vibration are what life is all about.*

*Most people are enslaved by their thoughts, thereby creating by default (creation by way of an unconscious means). It simply does not occur to them that they can free themselves from the chatter of the mind.*

*Everyday life, for the multitude, seems to be fraught with worry, tension, anxiety and fear. Thoughts arise in one's mind that serve to reflect these outer feelings.*

*There can be no peace of mind, no stillness, when one is engulfed by such negativity, and, yet, inner peace is within reach of each and every individual.*

*The battlefield of the mind is merely the war that plays out between dark (ego) and light (mindfulness), a battle that everyone must conquer.*

*Such is the journey towards self-realization, a journey in consciousness, a journey in metamorphosis, the quest for self-transformation, the journey of an observer, the journey to freedom. Such is the evolution of man.*

*The world, then, becomes a projection, an extension, if you will, of our own mind as well as our thought processes. The thoughts we think result in what we see.*

*We can choose, therefore, to see an abominable, doom and gloom, world or we can choose to see a wondrous, beautiful and magnificent, world.*

*The war we are fighting is an internal one where the battlefield is our own mind and the emotions we feel, live, express, become the ammunition that is fired.*

*Everywhere we turn in the media, we are being bombarded with fear by way of video clips, audio clips and text. There are times when getting past this numbing fear feels like a complete impossibility.*

*I know because I was once there, manipulated and controlled by my fears and anxieties. This becomes the distraction, you see; the means with which to keep you embroiled in fear.*

*The first monumental step becomes the realization that this is indeed the reality, meaning the power mongers wanting to keep everyone frozen in a perpetual state of fear.*

*It is only when an individual has arrived at this cognizance level, that he (she) can then begin to release themselves from the deadly stronghold of the illusion that one is powerless.*

*As stated before, the world that you see, and experience, is naught but a reflection of your own mind as well as the mind of the collective; hence, if you are to change what you see and experience, you must change what you think, feel and live on a day to day basis.*

*It is imperative that you learn to live in alignment with your heart. This rising of your personal vibration will also add to the enhanced vibration of the whole, of the collective, of Mother Earth.*

*In continuing to place our focus and attention on the problems of the world, thereby adding to the negative collective viewpoint, we simply get more of the same.*

*There is but one question that you must ask of yourselves.*

*Is this what I want?*

*You have the power to experience and live your life the way that you want to see it.*

*Everyone has the same choice.*

*Once you have experienced living in alignment with the heart, which is an increased sense of unity consciousness, you understand that duality no longer exists, for you have been able to transcend the illusion.*

*You are the revolution; a revolution whereby you must re-learn to think for yourself by taking your power back.*

*When you send out negative thoughts and emotions, not only do they affect yourself on an immediate and personal level, but they also affect the collective mind, the mind of the whole.*

*Having shared this, all are responsible for the current planetary disasters, myself included. It is imperative that you begin to understand the gravity of this situation, for only then can you begin to make the changes that are necessary, that are conducive, that are pertinent.*

*Having accepted the fact that all are responsible, each must then begin to take ownership and responsibility for having contributed to the situation at hand.*

*Step away from the poor me attitude, humbly embracing the power that exists within. Energy always flows to where one places their attention.*

*You learn to become pro-active by controlling your thoughts and emotions. Speaking from the heart, feeling from the heart, living from the heart, is the means through which you can do so.*

*One's focus and attention needs to be placed on living from a heart based consciousness as opposed to an ego dominated consciousness.*

*One must learn to protect their thoughts from fear and guilt so that they are better able to remain focused on love, compassion, nonjudgment; knowing that this is the way.*

*Stop watching the news on television.*

*Stop reading the newspapers.*

*Concentrate, instead, on what you want, and what you want to be, as opposed to its negative counterpart.*

*Take the time to delve within.*

*Meditate.*

*Focus on choosing love, for you will always find refuge within your sacred temple.*

*When you come to the realization that you are a spiritual being having a human experience, in order to experience yourself fully, your vibration shifts and begins to rise to a higher state of consciousness.*

*The biggest thing we are here to do is work on our individual selves.*

*If we can remain positive, no longer contributing to the collective negativity, we will have succeeded at something so monumental, so powerful, so necessary, that others, upon witnessing our example, will be able to follow suit, should that be their choice.*

*You must reclaim your power, a power that has always been yours, but that you elected to give away, a power that involves discipline of the mind and an earnest desire to live in alignment with Source.*

The words written on these opening pages belong to an article that I wrote, and published, in August 2010; an article entitled *Getting Out Of Our Own Way*.

If there were any specific words, thoughts, and/or phrases that resonated with you throughout the reading, then this book is for you.

Perhaps this volume will become your bridge to a better life.

Fear can be external, meaning that it can be caused by something outside of yourself that you are strongly motivated to avoid.

Fear can also be internal, meaning that it can be caused by something inside of yourself to which can be linked a strong, negative emotion, by way of past experience or conditioning.

Fear is often related to cognitive and emotional states, ranging from anxiety to worry to dread, from terror to horror to complete hysteria.

Likewise, fear can range from mild caution and distrust to extreme phobia(s) and/or paranoia(s), which may invoke completely irrational delusions.

There are relatively few people on the planet who can say that they have not experienced *some* level of fear.

Most are also familiar with the flight or fight response; a response whereby you believe yourself to be in danger; a response that elicits specific physical and physiological responses, such as:

[1] a rapid increase in heart rate

[2] a rapid increase in breathing

[3] an almost immediate increase in perspiration

[4] decreased blood flow to the skin

[5] an immediate tensing of the muscles

[6] dilated pupils

[7] a rapid increase in blood pressure

[8] an increase in blood-sugar levels

[9] high adrenaline levels

A very powerful emotion, fear, for the most part, is learned.

The process of creating fear takes place in the brain. It is the hypothalamus that initiates (controls) the flight or fight response.

While there are components to fear that can be self-induced, it has also been said that fear can be an entirely unconscious process.

Fear is such a powerful emotion that it can often be exploited through fear mongering, meaning that "unneeded, ineffective, or overpriced insurance policies, safety equipment, automobile undercoating, protection services, defensive actions, medications, and military expenditures are willingly purchased by people who are intimidated by a wide range of doomsayers." [1]

Fear mongering refers to the use of fear to influence the opinions and actions of another, towards some specific end.

---

[1] Beaumont, Leland R. (2005) *Fear: Imminent Danger* article accessed on June 10, 2011 at http://www.emotionalcompetency.com/fear.htm

Generally speaking, a fear monger is someone who stands to gain power, influence or funding, by spreading fear through public relations methods (all in an effort to generate emotions like panic, doubt and anxiety). [2]

By complete contrast, a love monger is someone who stands to gain self-respect, happiness and well-being by spreading love, courage and laughter to the general populace, especially in these most challenging of times; likewise, these are the very individuals who are also willing to accept the differences in others, whilst still loving them. [3]

Let's face it … we have a tendency to fear what we do not understand. In short, *terrorism is so effective because fear is so powerful.* [4]

In the course of my research, I came across an unfamiliar term called shockvertising (a type of advertising that deliberately shocks and/or offends the audience); a form of

---

[2] http://www.urbandictionary.com/define.php?term=fear+monger
[3] http://www.urbandictionary.com/define.php?term=love+monger
[4] Beaumont, Leland R. (2005) *Fear: Imminent Danger* article accessed on June 10, 2011 at http://www.emotionalcompetency.com/fear.htm

advertising that can only be described as controversial, disturbing and explicit, mainly because, as strange as it may seem, fear sells.

Fear destroys [1] one's self confidence, [2] the ability to think clearly and rationally, [3] relationships and intimacy, [4] the ability to remain positive, [5] whole body harmonics, [6] desire, [7] hope, [8] ambition, [9] one's dreams, and [10] love.

Based on this short list, it is easy enough to see that, in essence, fear can, and often does, destroy one's desire to live.

Fear also serves to promote [1] extreme negative thoughts (that have a tendency to become completely derogatory, debasing and/or defamatory in nature) towards self and others, [2] worry, [3] doubt, [4] feelings of inadequacy, [5] a sense of failure, [6] complete indifference, [7] total cowardice, [8] a state of inaction (whereby one does absolutely nothing), [9] a total neglect of self, and [10] violence.

If left completely unchecked, fear can, and will, destroy everything.

There is no life to be had when one exists within a perpetual (controlling) state of fear.

You need to become aware of the fact that the media, for the most part, is incredibly biased.

You also need to become aware that the media often *deliberately* creates fearful broadcasts (containing both accurate information as well as disinfomation) as a means of power and control (in that they are often mandated to report what gets reported, depending on who owns the news station).

The following bullets, as paraphrased from the work of David Icke, are of monumental importance. Please take the time to really think about them.

• Why is this information being presented to you?

• What is their *real* (and often hidden) agenda?

• Is it a case of problem – reaction – solution, meaning that *they create a problem* and *we react as they intend*, thereby asking for a fix?

• Do *they*, then, offer a solution?

• Might this *solution* be what *they* really wanted in the first place?

The real power lies with the multitude (meaning you and me), so please do not allow yourself to be fooled. Infinite power exists within every single individual. You have the power to decide your own destiny, but only if you do not give that power away.

When something happens that we do not like, why is it that we have a tendency to look for *someone else* to blame?

When there is a problem in the world, why is it that we have a tendency to wonder what *they* are going to do about it?

In retrospect, it is this type of non-action response that has resulted in the giving away of our power.

The same institutions and organizations that control the world, on a global level, want to control your mind because when they have succeeded in doing this (when you are no longer thinking for yourself), they have you where they want you; hence, the answer lies in taking your mind back, thinking for yourself, questioning what you are being told in an attempt to redefine your own truth(s), while also allowing others to do the same (without judgment or ridicule).

On a personal note, there are times when fear can also be your friend, as strange as that may seem. These situations might involve utilizing fear to force you into taking necessary action, thereby motivating you to make your life better in some way. It is in this manner, then, that fear can also guide you towards what you deem to be really important.

Fred Burks [5] talks about several core issues and their associated fears, namely;

---

[5] Burks, Fred. *Transform Fear Through Core Issue Work* article accessed on June 29, 2011 at http://stevebeckow.com/2011/02/fred-burks-transform-fear-core-issue-work/

[1] Abandonment – Nobody cares about me. I'm all alone. I don't matter.

[2] Arrogance – I'm better than all of you. I'm too much. I'm right and you're wrong.

[3] Damaged – Something is wrong with me. I'm a failure. I'm damaged.

[4] Inferiority – I'm not good enough. I'm stupid. I'm worthless. I'm boring. I'm hopeless.

[5] Rejection – I'm a burden. I'm unwanted. Nobody wants to spend time with me.

[6] Shame – I'm bad. I'm evil. I'm a mistake. I'm a monster. I'm disgusting. I'm possessed.

Many core issues, such as these, can often be traced back to instances in one's childhood.

They can be "a result of negative messages that were repeated many times to us by our parents or other significant people in our lives." [6]

It may well be that "one of these beliefs may have been driven deep into us during one or more traumatic experiences." [7]

In taking the time to explore your predominant existing fear(s), you can begin to transform your life for the better.

Possibilities, as per Fred Burks [8] include …

[1] Abandonment – I am worthy of love. I can find ways to safely share myself with others.

[2] Arrogance – I can learn from all around me. I can see goodness in everyone I meet.

---

[6] Burks, Fred. *Transform Fear Through Core Issue Work* article accessed on June 29, 2011 at http://stevebeckow.com/2011/02/fred-burks-transform-fear-core-issue-work/
[7] Ibid.
[8] Ibid.

[3] Damaged – I am whole and complete just as I am. I can choose to love all of me.

[4] Inferiority – I am a good, valuable person. I can make meaningful contributions to the world.

[5] Rejection – I am an attractive, interesting person. People can enjoy getting to know me.

[6] Shame – I can be gentle with myself. I can hold the best intentions for all deep in my heart.

Burks also shares that it is "a lack of acceptance and a deep feeling of being disconnected" [9] that lies at the core of these issues; a disconnection that can be "from ourselves, from others, from our spiritual nature, or from any combination of these." [10]

As you can see, it is imperative that you develop an acceptance of yourself and everyone around you.

---

[9] Burks, Fred. *Transform Fear Through Core Issue Work* article accessed on June 29, 2011 at http://stevebeckow.com/2011/02/fred-burks-transform-fear-core-issue-work/
[10] Ibid.

Likewise, you must also choose deeper connections for yourself.

You are not supposed to "avoid or suppress your fears and core issues. Working to accept and understand all parts of yourself, including your core issues, opens the door to transformation and allows you more easily, and naturally, to access your beautiful deeper essence." [11]

One key finding, in this line of work, is that "most people find that transforming fear through working with their core issues is like peeling away layers of an onion. You make a significant breakthrough, only to eventually find the same issue manifesting in another, more subtle form. Yet as each layer is peeled away, you will very likely find your life to be richer, more meaningful, and more enjoyable than it was before." [12]

---

[11] Burks, Fred. *Transform Fear Through Core Issue Work* article accessed on June 29, 2011 at http://stevebeckow.com/2011/02/fred-burks-transform-fear-core-issue-work/
[12] Ibid.

In essence, it is "by identifying and choosing to deal with our core issues, [that] we can transform our deepest fears and end up feeling more alive and more connected with ourselves and with those around us ... [which] then inspires us to participate more fully and effectively in building a brighter future for all of us." [13]

---

[13] Burks, Fred. *Transform Fear Through Core Issue Work* article accessed on June 29, 2011 at http://stevebeckow.com/2011/02/fred-burks-transform-fear-core-issue-work/

# Conditioning

We are socially conditioned, courtesy of our upbringing, to believe in, and become preoccupied with, a variety of topics, courtesy of [1] norms (accepted behavior) as inherited through the family, [2] customs (rituals and traditions) as adhered to by the family, and [3] ideologies (the shared belief of a group of people), all of which, in turn, formulate a set of ideas that form your goals, your expectations, your actions; thereby becoming your belief set, or mindset, if you will.

All of the aforementioned benchmarks (norms, customs and ideologies) involve a multitude of different social structures within established society; namely, education, employment, entertainment, popular culture, religion, spirituality, family life and the scientific community.

It is a combination of both society, as a whole, as well as peer groups that establish the norms, which, then, in turn, shape the behavior.

In referencing social conditioning, your mindset is usually focused on the limited ego conditioned perspective (meaning yourself, your family, your community, your country, your religion) as opposed to the expansive macrocosmic view (meaning cosmic consciousness, higher awareness, Christ consciousness).

In addition, the media also does a marvelous job of further curtailing your viewpoint, influencing you (the viewer) to commit yourself to increased materialism, needed or not, which also serves to maintain a more limited perspective.

Unfortunately, "the most common way to shrink someone's perspective is to put them into a state of fear. Make them feel their survival is threatened. Fear shrinks perspective. Fearlessness expands it. Fearlessness can take the form of unconditional love, service, transcendence, or even just curiosity." [14]

---

[14] Pavlina, Steve. (2006) *What Lies Beyond the Haze of Social Conditioning?* article accessed on July 1, 2011 at http://www.stevepavlina.com/blog/2006/03/what-lies-beyond-the-haze-of-social-conditioning/

When you come to realize that traditional media usually leaves you feeling far more fearful than fearless, you will come to better understand that "you become so accustomed to it [the fear] that you forget you're wearing it. You just conform to social norms and assume that it's the most intelligent way to live." [15]

By comparison, those who have "broadened their context beyond the scope of nationalism tend to behave very differently than those who still subscribe to the socially conditioned paradigm. For one, they aren't so easily manipulated, and they're more interested in long-term solutions than in placing blame or quick fixes." [16]

Let's face it.

We have all been socially conditioned by our parents, who, in turn, were also socially conditioned by theirs.

---

[15] Pavlina, Steve. (2006) *What Lies Beyond the Haze of Social Conditioning?* article accessed on July 1, 2011 at http://www.stevepavlina.com/blog/2006/03/what-lies-beyond-the-haze-of-social-conditioning/
[16] Ibid.

By definition, social conditioning refers to the process of inheriting tradition (which also includes a gradual cultural transmutation), one which is passed down through previous generations.

No matter your age, the most fundamental beliefs that you have about yourself and the world, at large, can be traced back to social conditioning.

In growing up, "our whole picture of the world is limited to our immediate environment, and so the way in which a child perceives the world is heavily dependent on the outlook of its parents, siblings, and relatives." [17]

There are functional families as well as dysfunctional families, meaning that some people grow up demonstrating (owning, manifesting) a  positive mindset, about all that life has to offer, whereas others grow up exhibiting a negative inclination.

---

[17] *Becoming Free of Your Parents and Social Conditioning* article accessed on July 1, 2011 at http://everydaywonderland.com/articles/becoming-free-of-your-parents-and-social-conditioning

That having been said, very few people are completely free of their unconscious social conditioning; that is, until they are able to recognize it for what it is, all in an effort to bring about transformational change within their own lives.

If you are not "fully at peace within yourself, and very few people are, chances are you will find it liberating to investigate your relationship with your parents, however supportive they were during your childhood." [18]

This soul searching, in an effort to learn more about the depths of the self, is a most important part of the enlightenment, or spiritual evolution, process.

There are countless beliefs involved when it comes to social conditioning.

In addition, conditioning can be overt (obvious and unconcealed) or subliminal (hidden and unconscious).

---

[18] *Becoming Free of Your Parents and Social Conditioning* article accessed on July 1, 2011 at http://everydaywonderland.com/articles/becoming-free-of-your-parents-and-social-conditioning

In the words of James Allen … *The more tranquil a man becomes, the greater is his success, his influence, his power for good. Calmness of mind is one of the beautiful jewels of wisdom.*

Learning how to dismantle your socially conditioned beliefs and attitudes (most of which you are completely unaware) in order to create profound personal transformation is *not* an easy process; it is a process that requires commitment, courage, awareness, as well as a willingness to face the truth about yourself. It is also an essential process for the individual who wants to evolve on a deeply spiritual level.

As a means of better demonstrating socially conditioned beliefs, let's focus on the negative beliefs affiliated with money.

[1] money doesn't grow on trees

[2] money goes out faster than it comes in

[3] money is evil

[4] those that have money are greedy and selfish

[5] it's wrong to want to be rich

[6] a penny saved is a penny earned

[7] only people who cheat have money

[8] money only comes from hard work

[9] I need lots of money to make more money

[10] we can't afford that

[11] I'll never have enough

[12] abundance is not my birthright

Concentrating on the flip side, let us see how vastly different the two worlds are.

[1] money is merely an energy exchange

[2] I'm the author of my own prosperity

[3] there's more than enough for everyone

[4] my prosperity does not detract from anyone else's

[5] the universe is an abundant place

[6] money is like water because it flows through your life and you direct the flow with your own intentions

In summation, money will play "the role in your life that you intend it to play, and that intention will largely arise from your pre-conditioned beliefs." [19]

If you've been conditioned to "associate negative qualities with money (especially through your upbringing), then money will play a largely negative role in your life." [20]

Likewise, if you "associate positive beliefs with money, then it will play a positive role." [21]

---

[19] Pavlina, Steve. (2010) *Is becoming Wealthy Inherently Evil?* article accessed on July 2, 2011 at
http://thebestofstevepavlina.blogspot.com/2010/12/is-becoming-wealthy-inherently-evil.html
[20] Ibid.
[21] Ibid.

Let's now focus on the negative beliefs associated with self worth.

[1] I'm not good enough

[2] I'll never be good enough

[3] I can't get it right

[4] I'm such a klutz at everything

[5] I'm worthless

[6] I don't matter

[7] I don't fit in anywhere

[8] I'm stupid

[9] I'm a complete failure

[10] I don't deserve to be loved

Reverse examples may constitute the following.

[1] I was born to achieve

[2] I create my own destiny

[3] My positive thoughts lead to positive actions

[4] All that I need already exists within

[5] I have permission to be exactly who I am

[6] I'm more than worthy of love and respect

[7] I'm unafraid to use my mind

[8] I trust my heart

[9] I celebrate both my diversity as well as my authenticity

[10] I will always remain true to who I am

[11] I strive for health and peace

[12] I believe in what it true to me

There also exist socially conditioned beliefs and responses when it comes to topics such as nationalism, patriotism, education, religion, race and gender, to highlight but a few.

Suffice it to say that "after years of growing up under the tyranny of ego, as expressed by your parents, the media, or society at large, you may have accumulated a heavy baggage of guilt and resentment." [22]

The most effective method for breaking free is by taking a deep and introspective look at your own conditioning.

What your parents "believe is best for you is usually a pretty clear reflection of their social conditioning, which in turn is the basis of your own social conditioning, and so your resistance to their advice is fertile ground for introspection. In fact, whatever suppressed grievances or resentment there may be in you towards them can hold the key to your freedom from suffering," [23] but only if met with unconditional love and forgiveness as opposed to resentment and defensiveness.

---

[22] *Becoming Free of Your Parents and Social Conditioning* article accessed on July 1, 2011 at http://everydaywonderland.com/articles/becoming-free-of-your-parents-and-social-conditioning
[23] Ibid.

If you are living on anyone else's terms but your own, "you are not fulfilling your primary purpose as a human being, which is to be of service to the heightening of consciousness. When you make decisions based on what you think other people want from you, or for you, life becomes devoid of beauty and spontaneity." [24]

Your ultimate purpose is "to live from truth, and to allow every single decision you make to come from creativity and intuition." [25]

When you first begin to awaken to the socially conditioned paradigm, it can be a very frightening experience, especially when you come to understand that "each individual working only for its self-interest ultimately contributes to the destruction of the whole collective." [26] Such begins the period of expansion that all will eventually experience, in their own time, in their own way.

---

[24] *Becoming Free of Your Parents and Social Conditioning* article accessed on July 1, 2011 at http://everydaywonderland.com/articles/becoming-free-of-your-parents-and-social-conditioning
[25] Ibid.
[26] Ibid.

In the course of the individual progress that is made, "the pain and fear will eventually subside. You will begin to feel more at peace. Your former life will be broken, but a new one will start to emerge. Once you acknowledge the trivial as trivial, you'll be ready to refocus your life on that which has the potential to matter. You will begin to seek out and embrace the real purpose of your life. And your new state of consciousness will begin to feel comfortable and even pleasurable to you." [27]

This is when you begin to function on a whole new level; a level whereby you can begin to "live as the fearless being you were always meant to be. Joy will become your natural state, and you will finally know what is important enough to live for." [28]

In essence, you are the architect of your future.

---

[27] Pavlina, Steve. (2006) *What Lies Beyond the Haze of Social Conditioning?* article accessed on July 1, 2011 at http://www.stevepavlina.com/blog/2006/03/what-lies-beyond-the-haze-of-social-conditioning/
[28] Ibid.

The choices and decisions you make right here, right now, serve to create your future.

The attitudes and beliefs that you choose to adhere to, right here, right now, serve to create your future.

You, alone, create the life opportunities of your choosing.

# Anger

By definition, anger refers to *a feeling of great annoyance or antagonism as the result of some real or supposed grievance, rage or wrath*, and can range anywhere from mild irritation to intense fury and rage.

Anger can be caused by both external events (traffic jam, cancelled flight, physical pain) as well as internal events (worrying about personal problems, self judgments, stress, anxiety, emotional pain).

In addition to how anger physically looks (a direct stare with widened eyes, grinding of teeth, clenching of fists, flushing of the face, tensing of muscles), there are some common physical effects that are experienced as well.

These include raised blood pressure, increased heart rate, and higher than usual adrenaline levels.

Like fear, anger has also been associated with the fight or flight response to pain, physical or otherwise, which also includes the threat of problems at a later date.

There are three main approaches to dealing with anger.

[1] Expressing your anger in an assertive (not aggressive) manner is the healthiest means.  To do this, you must learn how "to make clear what your needs are, and how to get them met, without hurting others.  Being assertive doesn't mean being pushy or demanding; it means being respectful of yourself and others." [29]

[2] Suppressing your anger, so that it can be converted and then redirected, is another method.  This happens when "you hold in your anger, stop thinking about it, and focus on something positive.  The aim is to inhibit or suppress your anger and convert it into more constructive behaviour.  The danger in this type of response is that if it isn't allowed outward expression, your anger can turn inward, on yourself.  Anger turned inward may cause hypertension, high blood pressure, or depression." [30]

---

[29] American Psychological Association (2011). *Controlling Anger Before It Controls You* article accessed on July 2, 2011 at http://www.apa.org/topics/anger/control.aspx (page 2)
[30] Ibid.

This unexpressed anger can also create other problems, leading to "pathological expressions of anger, such as passive-aggressive behavior (getting back at people indirectly, without telling them why, rather than confronting them head-on) or a personality that seems perpetually cynical and hostile. People who are constantly putting others down, criticizing everything, and making cynical comments haven't learned how to constructively express their anger. Not surprisingly, they aren't likely to have many successful relationships." [31]

[3] Finally, you can calm down inside. This means "not just controlling your outward behavior, but also controlling your internal responses, taking steps to lower your heart rate, calm yourself down, and let the feelings subside." [32]

Deep breathing (from the diaphragm) is a method that can be used in an effort to calm one's self. Hold the breath for a count of ten and then release, slowly, to a count of ten.

---

[31] American Psychological Association (2011). *Controlling Anger Before It Controls You* article accessed on July 2, 2011 at http://www.apa.org/topics/anger/control.aspx (page 2)
[32] Ibid.

Repeating a calming word or phrase (over and over again) works for some people. Likewise, imagery (visualization) is also a tool worth investigating.

Cognitive restructuring (a lofty term for changing the way you think) can also be a most effective means of keeping anger at a distance. Logic always defeats anger, because anger, "even when it is justified, can quickly become irrational. So use cold hard logic on yourself. Remind yourself that the world is not out to get you, [that] you're just experiencing some of the rough spots of daily life." [33]

While this is a technique that can be used, anytime, to develop a more balanced perspective, it is an especially effective tool to be used when you are angry.

Angry people tend to "demand things: fairness, appreciation, agreement, willingness to do things their way ... and when their demands aren't met, their disappointment becomes anger. As part of their cognitive restructuring, angry people

---

[33] American Psychological Association (2011). *Controlling Anger Before It Controls You* article accessed on July 2, 2011 at http://www.apa.org/topics/anger/control.aspx (page 4)

need to become aware of their demanding nature and translate their expectations into desires." [34]

In other words, saying, *I would like to be refunded* is healthier than saying *I demand to be refunded* or *I must be refunded.* While you will still experience the normal reactions (frustration, disappointment, hurt) when you are unable to secure what it is that you want, you will not feel the anger (to the same degree) as before.

Anger is a state of mind that often presents negative signs. It also needs to be pointed out that there is a way to channel the energy, associated with anger, in a positive direction.

While there are such things as anger triggers (things that just get under your skin), no individual or event "has the power

---

[34] American Psychological Association (2011). *Controlling Anger Before It Controls You* article accessed on July 2, 2011 at http://www.apa.org/topics/anger/control.aspx (page 4)

to make you mad. Anger is actually a choice, one that occurs depending on that person's perception (thought)." [35]

I also agree with Janet Pfeiffer, author of <u>The Secret Side of Anger</u>, when she shares that anger is not inherently negative. "It is an important and useful emotion that can be used as a motivating force to bring about positive change." [36]

In reflecting on the life of Martin Luther King, he was able to channel his anger, with respect to racial segregation and racial discrimination, into civil disobedience (often defined as nonviolent resistance).

Having visited Porbander, a coastal town which was then part of the Bombay Presidency (in British India) in 1959, he was very much inspired by Ghandi's success with non-violent activism.

As a result, he was the youngest person to receive the Nobel Peace Prize (1964).

---

[35] *The Positive Side To Anger* article accessed on June 22, 2011 at http://blog.beliefnet.com/inspirationreport/2010/05/the-positive-side-to-anger.html
[36] Ibid.

In truth, anger only becomes "a negative force when it is used in a destructive manner, either to hurt one's self, another or to damage property." [37]

In the end, the final decision always rests with you.

What will you choose?

---

[37] *The Positive Side To Anger* article accessed on June 22, 2011 at http://blog.beliefnet.com/inspirationreport/2010/05/the-positive-side-to-anger.html

Inaction can be described as *nonaction, deferral to another, quiescence, passivity, stagnation, laissez faire, idleness* and *inertness.* It can also be denoted as a *carefree, nothing to lose, live and let live* type attitude.

In short, inaction refers to a complete lack of action (which is *not* to be confused with stillness, as in finding peace without moving).

Inaction often refers to something that you want to do, as well as something that you feel you should do, but you do not carry it out (for whatever reason). [38]

Unfortunately, most of us have experienced inaction at some point in our lives; some have yet to graduate from this position.

---

[38] Schlegel, Dan. (2010) *Working to Overcome Inaction* article accessed on July 2, 2011 at http://www.danthatsrevolutionary.com/life/working-to-overcome-inaction

There are four main causes of inaction: [1] lack of purpose (vision), [2] lack of intention, [3] lack of self confidence, and [4] lack of accountability. [39]

In addition, fear can also bring about inaction.

Is it possible that one's ignorance could be directly related to inaction?

How about adding procrastination and indecision to that list?

Does not failure (which includes fear of failure) and self doubt also fit this same attitude environment?

It is clear that both over thinking and over analyzing are also a significant part of inaction.

Likewise, denial of one's identity will result in inaction as well as lethargy.

How about disinterest?

---

[39] *The 4 Causes of Inaction* article accessed on July 2, 2011 at
http://takethestairs.wordpress.com/2009/09/29/causes-of-inaction/

If you are being completely honest (as I, too, have had to be with myself), you will be able to see yourself in several of the previous examples.

Between feeling guilty, lonely, unworthy, not good enough, inadequate, fearful and judged, as well as feeling a lack of time, energy or commitment, any of these (and/or all of them) can contribute to feelings of inaction.

Inaction breeds doubt and fear. Action, on the other hand, breeds confidence and courage. How is it, then, that one can change their mindset from one of negative controlled inaction to one of positive conscious action?

The first step lies in both recognizing your state of inaction and then "figuring out what the worst that can happen from you not acting is, and also the worst that would happen if you do act." [40]

---

[40] Schlegel, Dan. (2010) *Working to Overcome Inaction* article accessed on July 2, 2011 at http://www.danthatsrevolutionary.com/life/working-to-overcome-inaction

This is where you attempt to create a positive (why) response for each negative (why not) thought.

The next immediate step becomes making a decision to commit to yourself (and that which you wish to create, through necessary change).

You are here to prove to yourself that you are quite capable of pursuing an idea, a goal, a dream.

In the words of Amelia Earhart … *The most difficult thing is the decision to act, the rest is merely tenacity. The fears are paper tigers. You can do anything you decide to do. You can act to change and control your life; and the procedure, the process, is its own reward.*

You must take responsibility for that which you want to have happen (create, materialize) in your life.

You must also act so that things happen as you want them to.

As Dan Schlegel shares, "the point of conquering inaction is so that you can act, and one of the major causes of inaction, from my observations and experience, is fear, so do that which you are afraid of and learn that it is really not terrifying at all." [41]

While this method may well work, you have to be mentally ready for this step. If you are not there yet, do not belabor the point as long as you remain committed to yourself.

Having a passionate goal, and being able to see it materialize within your mind's eye, is one of the best ways in which to overcome this state of inertia.

Start with just one goal, creating a picture, in your mind or on a vision board, that you wish to experience. Continuing to visualize the end result on a daily basis will serve to keep you focused.

---

[41] Schlegel, Dan. (2010) *Working to Overcome Inaction* article accessed on July 2, 2011 at http://www.danthatsrevolutionary.com/life/working-to-overcome-inaction

In using the vision board idea, you simply locate and cut out pertinent pictures (located in magazines) to paste on paper (cardstock, cardboard, display board), thereafter placing the board where you can easily reference it on a daily basis.

As you steadily work to imprint these images in your mind, there will come a time when you can actually see them in your mind's eye.

Mind Movies [42] is yet another way in which to create a vision board, complete with pictures and sound.

As the former British electronic band Faithless has so aptly written, *inaction is a weapon of mass destruction.*

With commitment, courage, awareness, as well as a willingness to face the truth about yourself, you can become humanity in action. It is in becoming a supporter of Humanity's Team that you also become part of a civil rights movement for the soul. [43]

---

[42] http://www.mindmovies.com/?10107
[43] http://www.humanitysteam.org/

Neutrality means the same as [1] *being impartial*, [2] *not allying yourself with any particular party and/or viewpoint*, [3] *the state or character (or policy) of being neutral (as in a dispute, a contest, nonparticipation in an armed conflict)*. It can also mean the same as *remoteness*, *disinterest* and *indifference*.

Every time I come across the term neutral, or neutrality, I quickly reflect back on my French Acadian ancestors who refused to take the oath of allegiance. Instead, the Acadians agreed only to an oath of neutrality, promising that if war broke out, they would not take up arms against France or Britain. In essence, they were taking an action of inaction.

When you are truly neutral, there is no good or bad, no right or wrong; instead, you are merely stating what is, without attaching any emotion to the situation. It is the same with energy. Inherently, energy is neither positive nor negative; it simply exists as energy … that is, until you attach some personal meaning to the energy itself.

It becomes your first priority, therefore, to stay neutral and own your individual space.

In demonstrating neutrality, however, so, too, must you demonstrate an increased awareness, otherwise when you "go into sympathy and take on responsibility for someone, it is possible you may match their energy level, get drained and lose your space." [44]

The core opportunity, in any situation that challenges you on an energy level, is to "stay neutral and get the learning; to stay aware of what is going on and to work on taking the charge off what is happening. It is so important to pay attention *when you start judging others* because that is when *your own issues have been triggered*. Most of the time when you react or strike back it is because you have taken something personally, it has hit an issue that needs healing. As a Spiritual Warrior, you need to notice when core issues are being triggered (lit up) in your space and avoid going into resistance or fight. This is great training for staying

---

[44] Robinson, Scott. *Neutrality* article accessed on July 3, 2011 at http://lsd.lightwork.ca/content/view/articles/234/77/

neutral. Notice whether you have taken offense. Are you hurt? Did you take something personally? Is your reaction because you felt like the person wasn't respecting you? Then, ask your higher self (your Source), what is the most appropriate action to take? When you are dealing with a difficult situation with someone by validating the person as Spirit, rather than invalidating what they are saying or doing, this will likely take the charge off the whole dynamic." [45]

From a spiritual standpoint, we are presented with opportunities, sometimes on a daily basis, from which to learn and evolve. Each time we judge another for their unique experience, we are unable to move forward.

Judging merely serves to invalidate both the authenticity as well as the divineness of each person.

Likewise, judgment is not a spiritual principle; it is a body dynamic.

---

[45] Robinson, Scott. *Neutrality* article accessed on July 3, 2011 at http://lsd.lightwork.ca/content/view/articles/234/77/

If we "lose our connection with our higher self, with Source, then the body will start to go off on its own," [46] even to the point of justifying whatever we do in the name of God or Source.

Holy wars, for example, are "based in competition and judgment, and have nothing to do with Source. The holy wars are about body wounds and power over others. As soon as you touch into a place of Spirit, of Source, you feel love for all sentient beings. All you want to do is heal and love. The idea that killing people can be involved as a way of being with Spirit, with Source, is ludicrous. It is simply judgment and all judgment is based on wounds." [47]

What you are here to learn (and remember) is that "making a neutral choice is not a judgment; if it has no charge for you, it is most likely clean and therefore a choice, not a judgment." [48]

---

[46] Robinson, Scott. *Neutrality* article accessed on July 3, 2011 at http://lsd.lightwork.ca/content/view/articles/234/77/
[47] Ibid.
[48] Ibid.

The act of "establishing power over others, as opposed to personal spiritual power, is a prevalent one in our world. It involves beings who are trying to find their power, but they do not know where to look, and so they push for power over others. They are trying to find what is missing ... [which is] their spirituality, their connection to Source." [49]

In truth, "spiritual wealth, spiritual wholeness, is the most complete, fulfilling thing there is. It is that connection with Source, and that wholeness spiritually, that every being on this planet is looking for, consciously or unconsciously, and transcending judgment is an important part of the process of finding those missing pieces." [50] In demonstrating neutrality, you are able to be with yourself (or another) in the now, simply observing without judgment, doing your utmost to remain "unpolluted by the thought-forms that encircle this earth, and hold you hostage." [51]

---

[49] Robinson, Scott. *Neutrality* article accessed on July 3, 2011 at http://lsd.lightwork.ca/content/view/articles/234/77/
[50] Ibid.
[51] Beckow, Steve. *Great White Brotherhood: Remain Neutral* article accessed on July 3, 2011 at http://stevebeckow.com/2010/09/great-white-brotherhood-remain-neutral/

It is imperative that you learn to "withhold your judgments by remaining neutral to the truths of others, [in order to] be tolerant for what you do not understand," [52] for the simple reason that the truth of one is not the same as the truth of another.

In remaining neutral to everything, so, too, is everything "being neutral to you. This is where you create a congruent and harmonious world." [53]

The ultimate question needs to become: do you really want to keep repeating the same lessons, over and over again, until you finally get it right?

---

[52] Beckow, Steve. *Great White Brotherhood: Remain Neutral* article accessed on July 3, 2011 at http://stevebeckow.com/2010/09/great-white-brotherhood-remain-neutral/
[53] Ibid.

Detachment refers to *disengagement, reflecting* and *pondering.* Apathy, by contrast, refers to *uncaring, coldness, coolness, stoicism* and *unresponsiveness.* As is clearly evident, considerable differences exist between these two terms.

When you are uninvolved, on both the mental and emotional planes, there exists a state of inner calmness. It is this very state that I am referring to when I speak of detachment.

People who possess emotional and mental detachment "can be very active and caring, though they accept calmly whatever happens. Such people accept the good and the bad equally, because they enjoy inner balance and peace." [54]

As you can clearly see, detachment, in this instance, does not mean indifference.

---

[54] Sasson, Remez. *Detachment and Being Detached* article accessed on July 3, 2011 at
http://www.successconsciousness.com/index_000066.htm

Have you ever given any thought to "how much time and energy are wasted every day, brooding on useless thoughts and feelings, due to lack of detachment? Much of the anger, frustration, unhappiness and disappointments [experienced] are due to lack of detachment." [55]

One of the ways you can work on developing detachment is through meditation.

In meditation, you do not interact with the thoughts and feelings that arise, thereby engaging the emotions. Instead, you acknowledge them, allow them to be, and refocus on simply breathing.

As you develop the habit of staying calm and emotionally detached during meditation, you will soon find that this skill also transfers to your everyday life. This is when you will find that you "feel and behave in a different way under circumstances that previously [would have] raised anger or

---

[55] Sasson, Remez. *Detachment and Being Detached* article accessed on July 3, 2011 at
http://www.successconsciousness.com/index_000066.htm

agitation. You will find that you can handle your daily affairs of life in a calm and relaxed way." [56]

Real detachment translates to "the ability to function calmly and with full inner control under all circumstances. A detached person is not harassed and hurried, and can do everything with concentration and attention, thus insuring a successful outcome of his actions." [57]

In the course of my research, I arrived at a remarkable site; one that more than adequately describes both attachment as well as detachment.

To begin, their opening was most catching ... *From the body we get the message of attachment. From the soul we get the message of detachment.* [58]

---

[56] Sasson, Remez. *Detachment and Being Detached* article accessed on July 3, 2011 at
http://www.successconsciousness.com/index_000066.htm
[57] Ibid.
[58] *Attachment and Detachment* article accessed on July 3, 2011 at
http://www.srichinmoy.org/resources/library/talks/human_experience/
attachment_detachment/index.html

From a spiritual standpoint, the body is limited in that it wants "to bind and limit our outer capacity and our inner potentiality." [59] By comparison, the soul is limitless and endless, meaning that it wants "to free us from the meshes of ignorance and liberate us from ... bondage." [60]

When we are detached, from both physical body as well as mind, we are able to supremely fulfill "our unlimited consciousness here on earth." [61]

In referencing both attachment and devotedness, they easily illustrate another significant difference in that "attachment is when we are in the finite, when we are attached to the finite," [62] whereas "devotedness is when we devote ourselves to the infinite and are liberated by the infinite." [63]

In truth, we are here to fully experience and live life.

---

[59] *Attachment and Detachment* article accessed on July 3, 2011 at
http://www.srichinmoy.org/resources/library/talks/human_experience/
attachment_detachment/index.html
[60] Ibid.
[61] Ibid.
[62] Ibid.
[63] Ibid.

To be involved with life, without egotistical attachment to an object (as well as an undertaking, an aspect of life, or a subject), this can easily equate to another definition for detachment (which also equates to Beingness).

Ray Posner shares that "detachment is a status of consciousness beyond the scope of mind ... [meaning that] those who function with the mind as the central instrument cannot hope to grow detached." [64] From a spiritual perspective, he further shares that detachment involves being engaged with life, while not attaching one's self, in an emotional manner, to circumstance, situation or outcome. Instead, it is imperative that a balance must exist between engagement, non-dependence and possession. [65]

In direct association with manifestation (as in the Law of Attraction), you must also relinquish your attachment to that which you desire.

---

[64] Poser, Ray. *Inner Detachment* article accessed on July 3, 2011 at http://www.gurusoftware.com/gurunet/knowledgebase/personal/SpiritualQualities/Detachment.htm

[65] Ibid.

This does not mean that you give up the intention to create your desire. What you must give up, instead, is your attachment to the result.

This denotes total and complete power in that "the moment you relinquish your attachment to the result, combining one-pointed intention with detachment at the same time, you will have that which you desire." [66]

When we have a problem that we have not been able solve, a problem that seems insurmountable, for example, we tend keep worrying about it.

In truth, this only energizes the problem, "giving it greater strength. However, if we forget the problem, we build up psychological strength, which causes life to cancel the difficulty. Thus, if instead of dwelling on the fact that we are poor, or are in debt, or a failure, or are ill, we ignore it, we attract conditions that are its opposite ... [while] this

---

[66] Poser, Ray. *Inner Detachment* article accessed on July 3, 2011 at http://www.gurusoftware.com/gurunet/knowledgebase/personal/SpiritualQualities/Detachment.htm

might seem counterintuitive to a rational mind, [it] is a proven spiritual principle of life that works, unfailingly." [67]

In short, when we "turn down the heat of our emotions in such situations, and practice detachment, withdrawing our intensity toward the issue, our negative energies dissolve, [thereby] enabling higher Forces to spring into action and work in our favour." [68]

In committing yourself to detached involvement, you are granting yourself the freedom to be as you are; likewise, for those around you. As uncertain as you may feel, know that this uncertainty is ultimately your path to freedom.

It becomes in remaining open to an infinite number of choices, that you are able to fully experience all the fun, adventure, magic and mystery that life has to offer.

---

[67] Poser, Ray. *Inner Detachment* article accessed on July 3, 2011 at http://www.gurusoftware.com/gurunet/knowledgebase/personal/SpiritualQualities/Detachment.htm
[68] Ibid.

From a cosmic perspective, "Beingness is the stability and calm behind all things. One approach [to Beingness] is to practice the technique of non-reaction" [69] meaning that "when any form of intensity comes our way, whether from another person or from the conditions of life, we simply do not respond [in an emotionally entangled manner]. This not only brings a level of peace to the atmosphere, but [also] attracts positive conditions." [70]

Beingness can also be denoted as "the ability to look out on the world as a Silent Witness, observing all that occurs through calm detachment. You care about what is before you; you consider it mindfully; but you remain stationed within as silent witness to all. In that state, you do not initiate or assert, but wait for life to take the initiative," [71] responding as you feel directed.

---

[69] Poser, Ray. *Inner Detachment* article accessed on July 3, 2011 at http://www.gurusoftware.com/gurunet/knowledgebase/personal/SpiritualQualities/Detachment.htm
[70] Ibid.
[71] Ibid.

As you try to "refrain from expressing a thought or opinion, allowing others to speak first," [72] this will enable "the flow of events to take their right course. This is to practice a form of restraint known as Silent Will." [73]

Beingness implies not immediately gravitating towards the negative, thereby avoiding wrong action. One example refers to an ability to "view a problem or challenge outside one's self and not complain about it. Complaining is a sign of a wanting attitude, psychological weakness, and wrong response. A spirit-oriented individual, on the other hand, gains power from right attitude, inner strength, and positive response, not complaint or grievance. Therefore, the next time you feel the urge to blame someone for something, restrain yourself. Not only will you create a more

---

[72] Poser, Ray. *Inner Detachment* article accessed on July 3, 2011 at http://www.gurusoftware.com/gurunet/knowledgebase/personal/SpiritualQualities/Detachment.htm
[73] Ibid.

harmonious atmosphere, but powerful positive conditions will [also] present themselves." [74]

Beingness also refers to accepting, and embracing, without challenge, whatever comes your way. At each point that "we embrace the given conditions of life, we move to a higher plane and open to the infinite potentials of life." [75]

In accepting all that comes to you, you are embracing the universe of possibilities, and moving from your "limited domain to a wider sphere where ... hopes and dreams are realized. It is to shift from the turbulence of life to the stillness and stability within. It is to express the spiritual dimension of Being in our everyday lives, attracting extraordinary circumstance from the world around us." [76]

I am trusting that you, the reader, are beginning to both understand, and connect with, the monumental importance of Beingness (along with detachment).

---

[74] Poser, Ray. *Inner Detachment* article accessed on July 3, 2011 at http://www.gurusoftware.com/gurunet/knowledgebase/personal/SpiritualQualities/Detachment.htm
[75] Ibid.
[76] Ibid.

When you are fully present in the moment (a process that also involves surrendering, in complete and total oneness, to the moment), there is a higher, spiritual, cosmic intelligence within you that begins to emerge, much like the chrysalis that emerges during metamorphosis; an intelligence that results "in true detachment: detachment from the future and past, and the emotions related to them." [77]

If properly detached, you are not worried about success.

If properly detached, you are not worried about losing.

Instead, you are here to simply enjoy the process involved.

By comparison, apathy refers to heedlessness and complete indifference; a state whereby all emotions (such as concern, excitement, motivation and passion) are suppressed.

---

[77] Nadadur, Desika. *Detachment versus Indifference* article accessed on July 4, 2011 at
http://www.desikanadadur.com/blog/2007/03/16/detachment-versus-indifference/

Likewise, apathetic individuals, are lethargic; they tend to exist without meaning in their lives (often feeling as if they have no sense of purpose).

Boredom and depression are also side effects of apathy.

Getting things done during the day has no recompense for them.

They are not interested in learning new things, nor are they open to new experiences; things just don't get done.

Clearly, suffering from apathy prevents one from living their life to the fullest.

Knowledge can be referred to as *information gleaned from a multitude of sources* as in cognition as well as through exoteric (which means communicated to the general public: familiar, known and evident) means.

Wisdom, on the other hand, can be referenced as *applied* (lived) *information* such as consciousness as well as through esoteric (which means understood by, and meant for, a select few who have special knowledge or interest: hidden, mysterious, mystical and arcane) means.

Ardriana Cahill puts it thusly ... "Knowledge is but the messenger that calls you to wisdom, but it is not wisdom. One can gain knowledge, but one does not seek wisdom; one meets it when one often least expects it and recognizes it as kindred. Knowledge puts us in the way of wisdom, but wisdom is experiential; it is a truth one recognizes in the external world that already resides in the internal one. One cannot learn wisdom; one must awaken to it." [78]

Based on the comparative opening at the beginning of this chapter, knowledge is intellectually based when contrasted with wisdom, which, located within, is divine.

In the words of our brother, Yeshua ben Yosef, the one we have come to know as Jesus, "Seek ye knowledge and ye shall find the truth that liberates. Seek ye discipline in the persisting with positive thoughts. Seek ye the joy of creating, the joy of learning, the joy of experiencing. Seek ye the realm of infinite possibilities for therein ye shall find the all. Seek ye the seer that ye be." [79]

Would you define these words as knowledge or wisdom?

Clearly, the more you seek knowledge (all knowledge), the more wisdom you will experience.

---

[78] *Knowledge versus Wisdom* article accessed on July 17, 2011 at http://www.controverscial.com/Knowledge%20vs%20Wisdom.htm
[79] Doucette, Michele. (2010) *Veracity At Its Best* (p 141). McMinnville, TN: St. Clair Publications.

Ardriana talks about the fact that knowledge and wisdom make use of two completely different organs when needing to communicate with you. "One is known, the other felt. The divine speaks to us through the spirit, not the mind. When wisdom is revealed to you (it does not explain itself), it reveals itself full blown, like manna from heaven on a silver platter. It awakens within as an all encompassing flood of warm illumination or a bolt of lightning that shocks or stuns you. This is why the sages call it enlightenment. Wisdom does not need digesting, deliberating, debating or dissecting by doubt or reason; it breathes within you as calm surety and perfect peace. It is then that you recognize [on an intellectual level], that this [inner knowing] has always been with you, just waiting for you to find it. From head to toe, you have everything you need to become extraordinary." [80]

The Vedas are a large body of texts, long preserved in ancient India, that constitute the oldest authority of Sanskrit literature. They are also the oldest Hindu scriptures.

---

[80] *Knowledge versus Wisdom* article accessed on July 17, 2011 at http://www.controverscial.com/Knowledge%20vs%20Wisdom.htm

While their exact date is controversial, it is quite possible that this knowledge dates back 10,000 years BC, meaning that they "were first written around 3,000 BC." [81]

The metaphysical foundation of Hinduism, as expressed in both the Vedas and the Upanishads, is "that reality (Brahman) is One or Absolute, changeless, perfect and eternal. The ordinary human world of many separate and discrete (finite) things (which our mind represents by our senses) is an illusion. Through meditation and purity of mind, one can experience their true Self which is Brahman, God, the One infinite eternal thing, which causes and connects the many things. True enlightenment is self-realisation, to experience the supreme reality as Self." [82]

Hence, while you live, "you are the caretaker of the divine within you." [83]

---

[81] *Ancient Eastern Philosophy* article accessed on July 17, 2011 at http://www.spaceandmotion.com/buddhism-hinduism-taoism-confucianism.htm

[82] Ibid.

[83] *Knowledge versus Wisdom* article accessed on July 17, 2011 at http://www.controverscial.com/Knowledge%20vs%20Wisdom.htm

It becomes through knowledge and wisdom that we are able to "eliminate fear, which produces understanding. We begin to understand who we are and why we are here. We recognize, with generosity, others stumbling while seeking their way, and develop a keen awareness and love for the miracle that is all Life, and that includes oneself." [84]

In essence, wisdom is a lifelong experience. While you must seek knowledge in order to reawaken wisdom, it soon becomes apparent that the more we know, the more we realize how much we don't know. Likewise, "the wiser we grow, the more wisdom we sense is yet to be discovered. With each step, we grow larger in each other's sight, we grow larger in the sight of the gods, and, it follows, the gods grow larger within us. Experiencing this knowledge, we find true humility and peace from the inside out." [85]

Knowledge changes over time. Wisdom is timeless.

_____

[84] *Knowledge versus Wisdom* article accessed on July 17, 2011 at http://www.controverscial.com/Knowledge%20vs%20Wisdom.htm
[85] Ibid.

Knowledge, gathered from learning and education, is often referred to as one's intelligence. Wisdom is intuitive information (as in inner knowing, words that may come to you, visions and gut feelings). As such, wisdom is unlimited, coming together, courtesy of personal experience.

While knowledge (in the form of gathered data and pieces of information) does not exist merely to serve wisdom, given its correlation with lifelong experience, wisdom, on the other hand, can be further enhanced through knowledge.

However, it seems to me as if each is connected on an even deeper level in that ... *knowledge becomes wisdom only after it has been put to practical use,* [86] thereby requiring active participation and action.

Mind you, without wisdom, knowledge can become dangerous, leading to conceit and selfishness.

---

[86] http://www.indiadivine.org/audarya/advaita-vedanta/142414-some-quotes-knowledge-wisdom.html

This is why it becomes essential to "use your intellect and your cognitive processes, as well as the wisdom that comes from your intuitive knowledge. The combination of these aspects is a powerful one, and will show you the truth that is right for you." [87]

In most cases, it will be your heart leading the way.

---

[87] Bendriss, Lilli and Løken, Camillo. (2011) *The Shift in Consciousness* (p. 13). Milton Keynes, UK: Lightning Source UK Ltd.

Everything is comprised of energy. Everything is vibration. All vibration is the result of energy in motion. Energy is held together to create matter. Matter is energy condensed to a slow vibration.

Everything in the universe has a unique vibrational energy. Every object, every being, every thought, every action, every psychological mood; in short, *energy equals vibration*.

Energy and vibration are what life is all about. We feel the energy (life force) inside our bodies on a daily basis, just through the wonder of breathing.

The electromagnetic grid of the Earth has a strong influence on human consciousness, meaning that any change in the grid "will have a corresponding effect on the consciousness of mankind." [88]

---

[88] Rennison, Susan Joy. (2008) *Tuning the Diamonds: Electromagnetism and Spiritual Evolution* (p. 69). Staffordshire,UK: Joyfire Publishing.

Ancient cultures were amazingly aware that every 26,000 years or so, the Earth makes a rare alignment with the center of our Milky Way galaxy.

It is understood that "when these alignments occur, they offer spiritual renewal for humanity, a transformation or evolution of consciousness." [89] Based on Mayan information, the next alignment has been predicted for December 21, 2012, a time that the Mayan elders see as the beginning of a new era.

In accordance with the research of Dr. Valerie Hunt, all healing takes place in the electromagnetic field. She also claims that as we come to "understand more of our electromagnetic nature and how to raise our frequency level, this will hasten spiritual enlightenment, which is our evolutionary goal." [90]

---

[89] Rennison, Susan Joy. (2008) *Tuning the Diamonds: Electromagnetism and Spiritual Evolution* (p. 58). Staffordshire,UK: Joyfire Publishing.
[90] Ibid, p. 108.

This means that as we "acknowledge our electromagnetic field and learn how to enhance it, we can undergo an evolution of consciousness, creating health and healing in the process." [91]

Likewise, our energy signatures (based on our levels of vibrational frequency) are also directly related to our level of consciousness. In turn, such is reflected in both mind and body.

The physical heart "is the most powerful generator of electromagnetic energy in the human body." [92] In fact, the electrical field of the heart "is about 60 times greater in amplitude than the electrical activity generated by the brain. Furthermore, the magnetic field produced by the heart is more than 5,000 times greater in strength than the field generated by the brain." [93]

---

[91] Rennison, Susan Joy. (2008) *Tuning the Diamonds: Electromagnetism and Spiritual Evolution* (p. 108). Staffordshire,UK: Joyfire Publishing
[92] Ibid, p. 124.
[93] Ibid.

In keeping, it is the heart that governs the emotions, as well as the health of the physical body, as opposed to the brain.

Emotions that occur in the frequency band of love (which include terms like appreciation, wonder, joy, compassion, gratitude, elation, encouragement, exuberance, peace, bliss) possess "this unique, most powerful, oscillating ability. Therefore, a loving heart can, and will, entrain other hearts/minds and affect those in close proximity by virtue of the force of its energy output. This research highlights the power of being loving to affect our own well-being and, it seems, those around us." [94]

The heart, then, demonstrates that, as an organ, it has a major balancing effect on the body. As a result, the emotions and states affiliated with love (as denoted above) vibrate at a higher calibration of consciousness.

This, then, is the key to health, healing and change.

--------

[94] Rennison, Susan Joy. (2008) *Tuning the Diamonds: Electromagnetism and Spiritual Evolution* (p. 126). Staffordshire,UK: Joyfire Publishing.

Positive emotions create "increased harmony and coherence in heart rhythms and improved balance in the nervous system. The health implications are easy to understand. Disharmony in the nervous system leads to inefficiency and increased stress on the heart and other organs while harmonious rhythms are more efficient and less stressful to the body's systems." [95]

In the esoteric tradition, the heart is considered "the gateway to higher consciousness." [96] What became even more fascinating for me was learning that it was the philosopher, Aristotle, who taught that "the seat of human consciousness lies not in the brain, but in the heart." [97]

Science, it seems, is now able to demonstrate what the mystics have always known; namely, the fact that the heart is pivotal to the practice of real spiritual life.

_____

[95] Rennison, Susan Joy. (2008) *Tuning the Diamonds: Electromagnetism and Spiritual Evolution* (p. 129). Staffordshire, UK: Joyfire Publishing.
[96] Ibid.
[97] Ibid.

In the words of the Hopi elders … *When the heart of man and the mind of man become so distant that they are no longer one, Earth heals itself through the catastrophic events of change.* [98]

Everything starts with consciousness. In fact, it has even been proposed that the electromagnetic field of the brain *is* consciousness. Likewise, the field of science has also been able to prove that we are able to interact with energy, meaning the Zero Point Energy field. It is now becoming more evident, courtesy of this knowledge, that space "was never an empty vacuum, but a vibrant mass of energy," [99] through which we are all connected, by way of both individual as well as planetary electromagnetic fields.

There is a solution to the issue of the current Earth changes and that means that we need "to teach people to change their consciousness." [100]

---

[98] Rennison, Susan Joy. (2008) *Tuning the Diamonds: Electromagnetism and Spiritual Evolution* (p. 161). Staffordshire,UK: Joyfire Publishing.
[99] Ibid, p. 161.
[100] Ibid, p. 165.

Our consciousness evolves when we "learn to develop our feeling nature without using judgment, so our feelings become just neutral reports of our awareness." [101]

Compassion is who you are.

The keys to compassion lie in your ability to embrace *all* experiences as part of the one, without judgment.

This is the greatest challenge that all must face as they move towards greater states of personal mastery, which is the return to their truest form.

Demonstrating love through compassionate allowing means that you must love others enough to *allow the range* of their experience.

Compassion is what you allow yourself to Become.

Compassion is your birthright.

Compassion is your truest nature.

---

[101] Rennison, Susan Joy. (2008) *Tuning the Diamonds: Electromagnetism and Spiritual Evolution* (p. 184). Staffordshire,UK: Joyfire Publishing.

Compassion allows you to view from an equal standpoint.

There is no judgment.

All people express their own versions of compassion through the manner in which they conduct themselves in every waking moment.

Are you willing to forgive those who have wronged you?

Are you willing to see beyond hate towards those who oppress you?

It is only in answering yes to these questions that *you can choose to Become more* than the circumstances.

In breaking the cycles of collective response, you become the higher choice.

Mastery of compassion means redefining what your world means to you.

It is *not* about forcing change upon the world around you.

You, and only you, choose how you respond.

As a being of compassion, you are offered the opportunity to *transcend polarity while still living within the polarity*. This is what enables you to move forward with life, a life filled with freedom, resolution and peace.

Compassion means living in trust.

Compassion means living with joy.

As your own vibrational level raises, so, too, are you adding to the increased vibrational level of the planet. By sending out "stronger, clearer messages in a loving, gracious way, we create a stronger, clearer reality." [102]

Balance equals order; hence, greater balance will bring greater internal order, all of which comes to be reflected in your outer world. Despite what appears to be happening, you must continue to withhold judgment, keeping all negative thoughts and feelings at bay (as much as is possible), primarily for the betterment of yourself.

---

[102] Rennison, Susan Joy. (2008) *Tuning the Diamonds: Electromagnetism and Spiritual Evolution* (p. 189). Staffordshire,UK: Joyfire Publishing.

Knowing that your thoughts create what happens in your life, and in your world, knowing that everything you do affects everything else in this universe ... this is why it has become even more imperative that you continue to believe in who you are, acting, always, on your convictions, your principles, your aspirations and innate experiences.

You must learn to adhere to your courage, your wisdom and your spiritual and moral integrity.

You must be willing to persevere against all unsightly odds. As you are able to keep your heart and consciousness in the right place, so, too, do you assist others in keeping with the same.

In knowing that you are here to learn your own lessons, so, too, are you here to respect that another is here to do the same.

It becomes in demonstrating both compassion and compassionate allowing (which is far removed from pity), that you are able to help yourself.

As you help yourself, so, too, are you able to help another, purely by example.

The reciprocal is also true: as you help another, you are, in truth, helping yourself.

As compassion deepens, "we find ourselves developing a nobility of the heart. Increasingly, and often to our surprise, we respond to difficult situations with calmness, clarity and directness. A quiet fearlessness or confidence is present as we no longer fear that we will compromise our own integrity. We find, too, a joy, a joy which arises from the knowledge that our every act is meaningful and helpful to the world." [103]

In touching the lives of others, in caring, compassionate and considerate ways, can it not be said that we are all angels?

---

[103] McLeod, Ken. *Awakening Compassion* article accessed on July 17, 2011 at http://www.unfetteredmind.org/articles/compassion.php

On the surface of our world right now

There is war, violence, and craziness

And things may seem dark.


But calmly and quietly

At the same time

Something is happening underground.


An inner revolution is taking place

And certain individuals

Are being called to a higher light.


It is a silent revolution

From the inside out

From the ground up.

## Getting Out Of Our Own Way

This is a global co-operation

That has sleeper cells in every nation

It is a planetary Spiritual Conspiracy.


You won't likely see us on TV

You won't read about us in the newspaper

You won't hear from us on the radio.


We are in every country and culture of the world

In cities, big and small, mountains and valleys

In farms and villages, tribes and remote islands.


Most of us work anonymously

Seeking not recognition of name

But profound transformation of life.


Working quietly behind the scenes

You could pass by one of us on the street

And not even notice.

## Getting Out Of Our Own Way

We go undercover

Not concerned for who takes the final credit

But simply that the work gets done.


Many of us may seem to have normal jobs

But behind the external storefront

Is where the deeper work takes place.


With the individual and collective power

Of our minds and hearts

We spread passion, knowledge, and joy to all.


Some call us the Conscious Army

As together

We co-create a new world.


Our orders come from the Spiritual Intelligence Agency

Instructing us to drop soft, secret love bombs

When no one is looking.

Poems ~ Hugs ~ Music

Photography ~ Smiles ~ Kind words

Movies ~ Meditation and prayer ~ Dance ~ Websites

Social activism ~ Blogs ~ Random acts of kindness ......

We each express ourselves

In our own unique ways

With our own unique gifts and talents.

*Be the change you want to see in the world*

Is the motto that fills our hearts

We know this is the path to profound transformation.

We know that quietly and humbly

Individually and collectively

We have the power of all the oceans combined.

At first glance our work is not even visible

It is slow and meticulous

Like the formation of mountains.

And yet with our combined efforts

Entire tectonic plates

Are being shaped and moved for centuries to come.


Love is the religion we come to share

And you don't need to be highly educated

Or have exceptional knowledge to understand it.


Love arises from the intelligence of the heart

Embedded in the timeless evolutionary pulse

Of all living things.


*Be the change you want to see in the world*

No one else can do it for you

Yet don't forget, we are all here supporting you.


We are now recruiting

Perhaps you will join us

Or already have.

For in this spiritual conspiracy

All are welcome, and all are loved

The door is always open.


This piece, *Love Is The New Religion* (also known as *The Spiritual Conspiracy*) was written by Brian Piergrossi and excerpted from *The Big Glow: Insight, Inspiration, Peace and Passion* and is shared herein with permission.

While you can visit Brian's website [104] for additional information, please also take the time to watch the Spiritual Conspiracy video [105] on YouTube, set to music and containing the very lyrics shared herein.

In truth, unconditional, holistic love is the "answer to all of life's challenges. We are here on Earth to learn how to love ourselves and others. We are here to accept ourselves and others completely, and without judgment," [106] wherein the

---

[104] http://TheBigGlow.com
[105] http://www.youtube.com/watch?v=mM7KddDERd0
[106] *Spiritual Words of Empowerment by Owen Waters* article accessed on July 30, 2011 at
http://www.infinitebeing.com/0601/empowerment.htm

true secret lies in understanding "that there is a difference between an acceptance of the outer beliefs of a person and an acceptance of their inner essence; regardless of that person's outward belief system, and whether you agree with it or not, it is the inner essence of the person that you learn to recognize, love and accept." [107]

Love is the medium through which we were created. Love, then, is what we are. It is something that naturally flows through us, although many individual life experiences have dictated otherwise, causing many to become unsure and untrusting.

It is my firm belief that unconditional love *will* heal the world.

---

[107] *Spiritual Words of Empowerment by Owen Waters* article accessed on July 30, 2011 at
http://www.infinitebeing.com/0601/empowerment.htm

Selfishness has often been referred to as the inner enemy. Selflessness, on the other hand, is to be embraced as a dear, devoted, most notable, reliable and trustworthy, friend.

As taken from <u>The Children of the Law of One and The Lost Teachings of Atlantis</u>, a further comparative example follows.

"Do your beliefs further the manifestations of unselfish love, or inhibit the manifestations of unselfish love?

Do they breed anger, hatred and harm or tranquility, love and healing?

Do they make for a better life, or a worse life?

Do they make for a better world for others, or a worse world?" [108]

---

[108] Peniel, Jon. (1997). *The Children of the Law of One and The Lost Teachings of Atlantis* (p 61). Alamosa, CO: Network.

We live in a world that has created the illusion of separateness from the universal spirit. This, in and of itself, has become the basis for the creation of selfishness.

When one takes the time to ask such questions as ...

"How much harm has been done in the names of God, country or tribe?

How much horror and pain has been inflicted because someone has a different racial, national, tribal, class, or religious belief?" [109]

... such is indicative that one is *truly on the path* which, ultimately, leads to spiritual enlightenment.

As shared further by Peniel, "those who know not that they are one, act not as one. Those who act not as one, create not love, but suffering and disharmony. What you create, you receive." [110]

---

[109] Peniel, Jon. (1997). *The Children of the Law of One and The Lost Teachings of Atlantis* (p 61). Alamosa, CO: Network.
[110] Ibid, p 63.

In essence, the fruits of your acts will follow you to the end of your days.

Peniel states that when we talk about the state of a person's consciousness, "we are essentially talking about the state of their awareness of the world around them ... directly related to the way they view, interpret, understand, and interact with, everyone and everything around them." [111]

A person's point of view, therefore, is affected by "both the state of their consciousness, and their beliefs and programming. Beliefs and programming are usually in sync with a person's level of consciousness. However, consciousness is dominant, and if there is a shift to a higher or lower state, the new consciousness can alter and override a person's beliefs and programming in order to match the new level of consciousness." [112]

---

[111] Peniel, Jon. (1997). *The Children of the Law of One and The Lost Teachings of Atlantis* (p 65). Alamosa, CO: Network.
[112] Ibid.

Taking it one step further, "all things in the Universe are essentially made of the same stuff ... [meaning that they are] totally interdependent and connected. So we cannot be truly separate from the rest of the Universe, we can only be a part of it all. But we can think we are separate. We can believe we are separate. And then we act like we are separate. Having separate self consciousness doesn't mean that you are really separate, but it does mean having a total illusion of separateness from everyone and everything else in the Universe. And when a person truly believes they are separate, they naturally focus on themselves. And when someone believes they are separate, and they focus their attention, and their energy ... [this] naturally leads to selfishness; the BIG issue, the BIG problem of all problems; the only REAL problem. As silly and simple as it sounds, it is serious: simple selfishness is the root of all problems and evils that exist on Earth. This is one of the greatest, most important teachings to understand." [113]

---

[113] Peniel, Jon. (1997). *The Children of the Law of One and The Lost Teachings of Atlantis* (pp 67-68). Alamosa, CO: Network.

The ego, or sense of being separate, "is the knowledge of good and evil. In order for something to be good or evil there must be an individual I to reference as the subject of good and evil ... [meaning that] *good and evil are relative only to the individual ego.* The ego doesn't want us looking for God because when we find God, the illusion of being an ego will be destroyed. One cannot see God and continue to live as a separate person. Each and every day we will watch the mind carefully and destroy our divisiveness. We will stop separating and start uniting. We will stop hating and start loving." [114]

The only cure for suffering, which constitutes all problems that we are faced with in today's world, lies in losing separate consciousness and selfishness by regaining consciousness of our oneness with everything and everyone.

This can only be attained through unselfish love, taking the time to look to both Jesus and Buddha as important and living examples of compassion, kindness, caring, giving, sharing and harmlessness.

---

[114] Walker III, Ethan. (2003). *The Mystic Christ: The Light of Non-Duality and the Path of Love According to the Life and Teachings of Jesus* (p 49). Norman, OK: Devi Press Inc.

We must see the illusions of self consciousness, that we carry with us in our mind, and break them.

I see this as being a very exciting time.

In knowing that you create your own reality by the very thoughts that you think, the very words that you verbalize, the very actions that you employ, now is the time to learn to let go of fear and concentrate solely on the expansion of love and forgiveness.

In working with thought forms, stay positive. It is only in thinking positive thoughts that you continue to attract more positive people and positive events/happenings into your life.

In this way you become like ripples in the pond, creating a domino of positive effects in the world.

In totality, therein lies your extraordinary contribution to the world.

Mindfulness involves several diffcrent components; namely, [1] awareness of the present moment (participating in the now), [2] nonjudgmental observation (the ability to observe without criticism, condemnation or judgment), [3] impartial watchfulness (for the simple reason that it means merely perceiving without taking sides), [4] nonconceptual awareness (which means that you do not get involved with thoughts, emotions, concepts; you merely observe without reaction), [5] non-egoistic alertness (in that everything takes place without reference to the self), [6] goal-less awareness (you accept the present moment for what it is, without trying to accomplish anything specific), [7] awareness of change (which becomes obvious in the course of the observation) and [8] participatory observation (whereby you are both participant and observer at the same time; an alert participation in the ongoing process of living). [115]

---

[115] *Sati* article accessed on July 17, 2011 at
http://dharma.ncf.ca/introduction/instructions/sati.html

Despite these constituent parts, mindfulness still needs to be experienced in order to be fully understood.

Mindfulness, in short, is *a state of active, open attention on the present* (the here and now) *without judgment.*

One of the simplest ways to achieving mindfulness is focused breathing (from your diaphragm as opposed to your chest). You breathe in through your nose and out from your mouth. If you are able to focus on your breathing, in this manner, whenever you are stressed, agitated or upset, you will find the exercise both calming and grounding.

Listening to soothing music (classical, slow tempo, nature based sounds) and focusing on the sound (vibration) of each note, is also another wonderful way in which to experience mindfulness.

Believe it or not, cleaning the house, with an established positive mindset before beginning, can also assist one in experiencing mindfulness.

Whenever you become totally focused on completing an activity, whatever it may be, and enjoying what you are accomplishing, you have become a mindful participant.

Meditation still continues to be one of the most popular ways in which to achieve mindfulness.

Taking the time to step back and observe your thoughts (feelings, emotions) is another way to achieve mindfulness. This might be a wise alternative for those who find meditation to be too much of a challenge for them.

Instead of trying to combat the voice in your head, you simply sit and take the time to observe your thoughts without reacting to them in any way. You acknowledge them and then let them go, almost as if releasing a balloon to the wind.

A daily commitment to exercise can also work, especially if you take the time to focus on the muscles of the body and how they feel when to stretch, warm up, speed up, walk, run, jog, slow down.

Mindfulness is not about detaching from your experience.

Mindfulness is not about detaching from life.

Mindfulness is not about disengaging on an emotional level.

Instead, mindfulness allows you to engage more fully, with emotions and experiences, rather than simply reacting (which might also translate to over reacting).

Mindfulness, courtesy of the nonjudgmental awareness component, is not the same as accepting whatever happens (including things of a harmful nature).

Mindfulness is not about becoming a passive bystander to life.

Instead, *mindfulness allows you to respond* to events, people and situations *with enhanced awareness and thoughtfulness*.

The benefits to the practice of mindfulness are many; namely, [1] improvements in mood as well as health, [2] improved concentration (focus), [3] clarity of thinking, [4] enhanced (deepened) peace of mind, [5] significantly reduced stress, [6] improved intuition (which, in turn, further enhances both insight and wisdom), [7] increased self confidence, and [8] a more insightful awakening to authenticity (the real you), to make note of a few.

Like wisdom, so, too, is the cultivating of mindfulness a lifelong endeavor.

*The Peaceful Warrior* is a movie that deals with mindfulness in the present moment. I highly recommend that each reader take the time to watch this movie.

First off, let's break each word down individually.

Integral means necessary, essential, fundamental, requisite, intrinsic and indispensable; spiritual means pure, sacred, divine, mystical, metaphysical, and transcendental; practice means action, study and training.

Putting them all together, integral spiritual practice refers to *living one's daily life in a pure, unadulterated, meditative and mindful* (conscious) *manner.*

How do you cultivate such a practice?

First and foremost, you have to make an honest effort to eliminate stress from your life. When we are stressed, specific hormones, such as cortisol, GH and norepinephrine, are released.

Cortisol, a steroid hormone produced by the adrenal glands, is released in response to stress. While cortisol is an important part of your body's response to stress, it is also important that your autonomic nervous system functioning return to normal, as experienced through physiological relaxation.

In our current high stress culture, there are numerous instances whereby this does not happen, meaning that high and/or prolonged levels of cortisol have been shown to [1] impair cognitive performance, [2] suppress the function of the thyroid, [3] cause blood sugar imbalances, [4] cause high blood pressure, [5] lower one's overall immunity, and [6] increase abdominal fat (which is what can lead to heart attacks and strokes).

Exercise, yoga, listening to soothing music, meditation, guided imagery and focused breathing are all differing practices (herein considered integral spiritual practices) that have been shown to keep cortisol levels healthy and under control.

GH (growth hormone), as made by the pituitary gland, is also affected by stress. If a child is associated with a home environment involving serious marital discord, alcoholism or child abuse, their developmental growth can be impaired.

Norepinephrine is a hormone, secreted by the adrenal glands, that works with epinephrine (also known as adrenalin). Released when a host of physiological changes are activated by a stressful event, high levels of norepinephrine result in [1] an increased heart rate, [2] an immediate triggered release of glucose from the energy stores of the body, as well as [3] increased blood flow to the muscles.

In a body that may already be depleted in energy, constant stress leads to high blood pressure and stress induced hypertension. Likewise, increased stress levels affect the immune system, making it more susceptible to viral infection and disease.

In asthmatics, stress can cause severe constriction of the bronchial tubes.

Stress also increases the risk for diabetes, ulcers and plaque buildup in the arteries.

It is paramount, therefore, that you learn to control your stress levels considerably.

As stress levels are reduced, it becomes easier to let go of negative thoughts and emotions, thereby contributing to the development of a strong and positive attitude.

As the Beatles have stated, you have to learn to simply *let it be*, for *there will be an answer* within the stillness, within the solitude, within the inner reflection.

Stop watching the news before going to bed. Instead, try taking a bath, while listening to soft music or soothing and repetitive sounds (falling rain, waves, waterfall) in your attempt to enhance a restful sleep.

You cannot protect those around you, for they, too, must live their own experiences.

You are not here to dictate how another should live, for that limits your understanding of them. By direct association, this behavior also serves to limit their understanding of themselves.

You are not here to change anyone, other than yourself.

As you come to associate with other spiritual individuals who have similar mindful beliefs, you will find yourself living a more satisfying life.

It becomes in eradicating fear from your life that you allow yourself to live in love.

The ability to love and be loved is a most basic human trait. As a society, we have become incredibly disconnected from love, living with fear-based emotions (such as depression, loneliness, guilt, attachment and anger).

Finding ways to reconnect with others is tremendously helpful in developing a positive attitude.

Take the time to laugh well, laugh much and laugh often. It is important to find humor in the simplest of things. Likewise, laughter is an incredibly powerful mood elevator.

Getting back to the simple things in life, seeing yourself through the eyes of a child, becomes a liberating experience.

Take the time to reconnect with old friends. Take the dog for a walk. Watch a satisfying movie. Listen to your favorite music. Read a great book. Spend time with nature. Exercise on a daily basis. Truly, the simplest things in life give us the most pleasure.

Religions have had "a close relationship, not only with violence, but with economic exploitation. Indeed, it is often the economic exploitation that necessitates the violence." [116]

I am much more interested in a meditative and investigative discipline, one that is "intended to promote an inner harmony and enlightenment while directing us to a path of right living" [117] whereby the spiritual focus "is not only on oneself, but on the welfare of others." [118]

---

[116] Parenti, Michael. *Friendly Feudalism: The Tibet Myth* article accessed on June 27, 2011 at
http://stevebeckow.com/2011/01/michael-parenti-examines-dalai-lama-tibetan-buddhism/
[117] Ibid.
[118] Ibid.

Culture is "anything but neutral. Culture can operate as a legitimating cover for a host of grave injustices, benefiting a privileged portion of society at great cost to the rest." [119]

In short, there is a monumental "difference between a spiritual bond and human bondage." [120]

*Satsang* (*sat* means true, *sang* means company) is a Sanskrit word. This can easily be translated to I am my own true companion. Likewise for I am my own communion with truth.

I am my own theological, spiritual and philosophical mentor, for as I read spiritual (metaphysical, inspirational) works, both assimilating and meditating on their meaning, paying attention to the inner voice of guidance and teaching that has been awakened within, this brings enhanced truth into my daily life.

---

[119] Parenti, Michael. *Friendly Feudalism: The Tibet Myth* article accessed on June 27, 2011 at
http://stevebeckow.com/2011/01/michael-parenti-examines-dalai-lama-tibetan-buddhism/
[120] Ibid.

The nature and goal of *Satsang* is "to establish a direct, unbreakable communion with your Higher Self, while living an active worldly life." [121]

This is what comprises my personal spiritual practice.

---

[121] Satsang with the Self website accessed on July 22, 2011 at http://satsangwiththeself.com/

Discernment pertains to *being able to grasp and comprehend what is obscure* (not easily understood, concealed, cryptic, hidden). As a result, discernment is very much associated with one's perceptiveness.

The first step to change is, of course, discernment; noticing that I am doing it; thereafter, judgment, meaning that what I do with what I notice, becomes a choice. [122]

You can judge the authenticity of your discernment by the outcomes.

You will know that you have made the right decision because you are filled with an inner calmness or a deep abiding peace.

In effect, discernment usually comes down to feelings and intuition.

---

[122] *Judgment versus Discernment* article accessed on July 22, 2011 at http://www.superenlightme.com/judgment-versus-discernment

Discernment is also "more about paying attention to your inner voice [heart, intuition] than about analysis [mind]." [123]

It is the belief of author Mariana Caplan that we evolve spiritually "by cultivating discernment that is powerful enough to pierce through confusion on every level of our experience." [124]

In order to discern at such a pertinent level, there are several noteworthy steps.

First of all, we must be willing to *Let Go and Let God* by letting go of the fear associated with change (the unknown).

Next comes diligence; we must remain alert to becoming the objective bystander, confronting both past and present in order to affect a more cognizant future. We must learn to trust our intuitive selves, our inner guide, our Higher Selves.

Lastly comes mindfulness and compassionate allowing.

---

[123] MacLean, Kenneth. *Finding Your Spiritual Gift – Discernment* article accessed on July 22, 2011 at
http://wisdomalacarte.net/blog/finding-your-spiritual-gift-discernment/2011/04/
[124] http://realspirituality.com/pages/pdf/presskit_eyes.pdf

The degree to which "we are awake, conscious, and discerning in our experience and choices is the extent to which we can consciously participate in our soul's unfolding." [125]

It is imperative that you learn "to recognize and follow the more reliable guidance of the deeper aspect of the *real* you [which is] ... the Higher Self or Soul Self, [the] ... aspect of you that is beyond the constructed ego conditioning and conditioned response patterns." [126]

While there are 12 attitudes that serve to strengthen your discernment, helping you travel the spiritual path with greater clarity ... [1] sincerity of intention, [2] compassion, [3] vulnerability and openness, [4] patience, [5] equanimity, [6] responsiveness, [7] passion, [8] relaxation, [9] contentment, [10] a sense of humor, [11] wonder and openness to magic, and [12] humility ... do not expect to be

---

[125] http://realspirituality.com/pages/pdf/presskit_eyes.pdf
[126] Soul Insight 4 Spirit Led Living website featuring *Spiritual Discernment* article accessed on July 22, 2011 at http://www.soulinsights4spiritledliving.com/2011/05/spiritual-discernment.html

able to cultivate and express all at the same time, all of the time. [127]

You are *continually evolving and changing* as per your own individual experience(s). This also adds to both the greater collective experience as well as the totality of God, which means, as well, that *God is also continually evolving and changing*.

Likewise, your truth is ongoing, evolving, being created every moment by every thought you have.

While there is a paradox associated with truth, it is also a profound truth, no matter how contradictory it may appear.

When you have come to understand that *everything* is true and yet *nothing* is true, you shall be able to see that just as you perceive truth to be whatever you determine it to be, so may all.

---

[127] http://realspirituality.com/pages/pdf/presskit_eyes.pdf

In continuation of this explanation, in the moment that you no longer give credence to a truth, it is no longer real, for you have since moved toward a new truth.

When you come to understand that truth *is* and *can be* all things, then you are free, no longer enslaved to laws, rules, dogma or intellectual understanding.

To learn to Become multi-faceted in your truth means that you are not *one* truth, but *all* truths.

Rest assured that the inner wisdom and inner knowing, of which you seek, is there … to be found in the stillness that exists within.

Indifference can be described as *aloofness, carelessness, lack of interest or concern* and *complete disregard* for anything and everything, including human life.

According to Holocaust survivor Elie Wiesel, indifference is a word that, etymologically, means no difference. He continues by saying that indifference is "a strange and unnatural state in which the lines blur between light and darkness, dusk and dawn, crime and punishment, cruelty and compassion, good and evil. What are its courses and inescapable consequences? Is it a philosophy? Is a philosophy of indifference conceivable? Can one possibly view indifference as a virtue? Is it necessary, at times, to practice it simply to keep one's sanity, live normally, enjoy a fine meal and a glass of wine, as the world around us experiences harrowing upheavals?" [128]

---

[128] American Rhetoric Top 100 Speeches website accessed on July 22, 2011 at

He then talks about how tempting, and seductive, indifference can be in that "it is so much easier to look away from victims. It is so much easier to avoid such rude interruptions to our work, our dreams, our hopes. It is, after all, awkward, troublesome, to be involved in another person's pain and despair. Yet, for the person who is indifferent, his or her neighbor are of no consequence. And, therefore, their lives are meaningless. Their hidden, or even visible, anguish is of no interest. Indifference reduces the Other to an abstraction." [129]

To be indifferent to suffering, is what makes a human being inhuman. This, he says, is what makes indifference even more dangerous than anger, more dangerous than hatred.

While both anger and hatred may often elicit a response, "indifference elicits no response. Indifference is not a beginning; it is an end. And, therefore, indifference is always the friend of the enemy, for it benefits the aggressor, never his victim, whose pain is magnified when he or she

---

http://www.americanrhetoric.com/speeches/ewieselperilsofindifferenc e.html
[129] Ibid.

feels forgotten. The political prisoner in his cell, the hungry children, the homeless refugees – not to respond to their plight, not to relieve their solitude by offering them a spark of hope is to exile them from human memory. And in denying their humanity, we betray our own." [130]

*Because of indifference, one dies before one actually dies.* Elie Wiesel

There is also another way of looking at indifference, as in *judge ye not.*

In fact, the way to remembering the sacredness of all life is the way of nonjudgment.

As you become aware of your limiting beliefs and opinions, you come to understand that your interactions with others are driven by what *you believe to be true* about the person.

---

[130] American Rhetoric Top 100 Speeches website accessed on July 22, 2011 at
http://www.americanrhetoric.com/speeches/ewieselperilsofindifferenc
e.html

Sadly, these limiting beliefs *never* reflect the actual truth, a truth that states all is one.

As you gain in universal awareness, you quickly come to the realization that your divinity is also theirs as well.

When you respond to people with love and compassion, you readily move from conflict to harmony; such is the freedom sought by all.

While many continue to accept limiting thoughts, of which there are a significant number (including fear, guilt, despair, unworthiness, failure, worry, unhappiness, pity, misery, hatred, dissension, denial of self), into their lives, it must be remembered that this is neither good nor bad.

Coming from a place of nonjudgment, it simply is.

In the end, we must summon into mind that *everything comes down to personal choice.*

Patañjali was the compiler of the Yoga Sutras, a Hindu text and foundational scripture of Rāja Yoga (the cultivation of the mind using meditation to further one's acquaintance with reality, thereby allowing the individual to finally achieve liberation). Therein, *upeksha* is a word that means indifference without any attitude, [131] [132] [133] which clearly implies that you have no right to judge another for their experience(s). Who are you, then, to decide what is right and what is wrong for anyone other than yourself?

It is in becoming more mindful and aware, that you will also experience, firsthand, indifference without attitude.

The darkness is a most powerful catalyst. This is something that must be reconciled within each individual.

There are many feelings and emotions that find their root in the dark, those that you have come to know as fear, rage, anger, hate, jealousy, depression, control, violation, incest, suspicion, denial, pain, judgment, illness, disease, death, greed, bitterness and retribution.

---

[131]

http://www.messagefrommasters.com/oshoyoga/osho_joy_towards_the_virtuous.htm

[132] http://en.wikipedia.org/wiki/Pata%C3%B1jali

[133] http://en.wikipedia.org/wiki/Yoga_Sutras_of_Patanjali

The darkness is as much a part of you as is the light.

There is, however, a way to avoid the force of this darkness; a power which lies in making choices that do not embrace the dark.

Allowing darkness to exist does not mean that such has become your choice.

Allowing darkness to exist does not mean that you have condoned it.

Allowing darkness to exist simply indicates that you have acknowledged the existence of this force, a force that actually serves to remind us of the exact opposite.

Every event in life serves as a catalyst that moves us into new experiences of ourselves.

There is no good, no bad, no right, no wrong.

It has always been our choice to expand and know ourselves in all ways.

Allowing provides you with the opportunity to transcend the polarities of light and dark, a feat that you accomplish by embracing both as equal expressions of the same force from which we come.

When you come to understand that truth *is* and *can be* all things, then you are free, no longer enslaved to laws, rules, dogma or intellectual understanding.

Your ability to express forgiveness, allowing others the outcome of *their* own experiences, without changing the nature of who you truly are, is the highest level of mastery to which you can attain.

Therein lies the healing of all illusion, all separation, all duality.

Suppression can refer to such terms as *oppression, censorship, religious intolerance* and *thought suppression*. It can also refer to words such as *elimination, destruction, obliteration* and *complete annihilation*.

Suppression, then, can involve [1] *forcibly putting an end to something,* [2] *preventing something from being expressed or published,* and [3] *preventing or inhibiting a process or phenomenon.*

Unboundedness, on the other hand, means the same as both *total freedom* and *complete expansion*.

Let's face it; you can either approach transformation with a limited (unconscious and reactive) awareness or an expanded (conscious and proactive) awareness.

When you take a reactive approach, you are responding automatically and unconsciously to the dynamics of the situation.

130

When you employ a conscious approach, you are responding proactively. This means that you are able to demonstrate the ability to both witness the experience (as an alert and clear minded observer) as well as reflect (objectively) on the experience.

In short, *being conscious simply means that you are aware of being aware.*

As your awareness develops, "you become less attached to ideas, objects, and circumstances in your life. As your consciousness evolves you become more of an objective observer of life, and are less subjugated by wants, needs, or desires. You become more accepting and compassionate and less opinionated, reactionary, or resentful. Things just don't bother you like they used to, you become less emotionally vulnerable." [134]

Clearly, increased awareness becomes the foundation to mastery of the self, for it is simply the lack of awareness that has created so many problems.

---

[134] Manifest Messenger email series (as taken from *The Awakening* by Steven S. Sadleir) received from Jackie Lapin on June 20, 2011.

In order to become more conscious, more aware, thereby rising above the unconscious state, "you need to experience being alert and awake," [135] by becoming the bystander; the observer; the person who watches with astute objectivity.

When you are able to be aware of your own awareness "you will realize how cunning the mind is, and how great it is at rationalizing. Rationalizing is not awareness; *awareness means that whatsoever is happening in the moment is happening with complete consciousness*, [and] that you are fully present." [136]

The mind is only able to work linearly, meaning "from point A to point B, from one thought to the next. If you move vertically, that is a movement of consciousness, which is awareness." [137]

---

[135] Campuzano, Ivan. (2009) *How to Increase Your Awareness and Expand Your Consciousness* article accessed on July 27, 2011 at http://ivancampuzano.com/how-to-increase-your-awareness-and-expand-your-consciousness/
[136] Ibid.
[137] Ibid.

You must learn to "continually bring yourself to the present. When you catch yourself living in the past or imagining the future, bring your awareness back to the present moment. Do not feel bad when you realize you are not in the present, this is just a habit you need to gradually get out of until your new habit is being more in the present." [138]

By now, you will have figured out that life is constantly changing and evolving.

So, too, are you, constantly changing and evolving. It is imperative, then, that you learn to evolve into a more consciously awake being.

As you learn to live a more conscious life, all of the actions that you take, and the decisions that you make, coming from a heart based consciousness, will be "natural and perfect for the situation." [139]

---

[138] Campuzano, Ivan. (2009) *How to Increase Your Awareness and Expand Your Consciousness* article accessed on July 27, 2011 at http://ivancampuzano.com/how-to-increase-your-awareness-and-expand-your-consciousness/
[139] Ibid.

Not only that, but a person of awareness is "calm, relaxed, quite, serene, creative; only good can come from these states of being." [140]

Are you now able to see how enhanced awareness is linked with one's health and well-being?

How will you know when you have become a person of awareness? It will have become evident when you "quit watching others, that's what everybody else does; all you need to do is watch yourself." [141]

*Increased awareness*, then, *becomes the key to spiritual transformation.*

In turn, this is what is meant by total freedom and complete expansion.

---

[140] Campuzano, Ivan. (2009) *How to Increase Your Awareness and Expand Your Consciousness* article accessed on July 27, 2011 at http://ivancampuzano.com/how-to-increase-your-awareness-and-expand-your-consciousness/
[141] Ibid.

Transcendence means to be free from limitations inherent in matter.

Transcendence also means having continuous existence above and beyond the physical world as we know it.

Simply put, transcendence means the real self, the fully conscious self, the essence of who and what you really are.

Likewise, transcendence is also a self-mastery process that enables you to understand the differences between creating by conscious intent versus creating by default.

Transcendence pertains to living from a heart-based consciousness (love) instead of an ego-based consciousness (fear, guilt, power, control).

Here is the key to transcendence ... *to know something, you must become it.*

As denoted by many spiritual seekers, changing the way you think is what completely transforms your experience of living.

In the words of John Roger, founder of the Movement of Spiritual Inner Awareness (MSIA) ... *All that you want to be, you already are. All you have to do is move your awareness there and recognize the reality of your own Soul.*

The purpose of The Movement of Spiritual Inner Awareness (MSIA) "is to teach Soul Transcendence, which is becoming aware of yourself as a Soul and as one with God, not as a theory but as a living reality. Your Soul is who you truly are; it is more than your body, your thoughts, or your feelings. It is the highest aspect of yourself, where you and God are one." [142]

Knowing that there is much joy and beauty in life, what is it, then, that is keeping us from discovering this inner peace, this joy, this beauty, this total contentment?

---

[142] http://www.msia.org/soultranscendence

Unfortunately, we have only ourselves to blame when we worry and are fearful.

If we were to embrace any given situation with the calm acceptance of truth (without complaint, without a grudge, without surrendering or giving up), simply allowing the body to go with the flow (because it is what it is), we would have transcended this illusionary world of ego long ago.

When your mind completely transcends thought, you experience a state of restful alertness and inner peace.

This is what continues to be referred to as Transcendental Consciousness.

It has been said that the enlightened mind can attain and gain the true, transcendent type of free will but only by emphatically rejecting the false, deluded type of free will. [143]

---

[143] *Transcending Determinism: Transcendent Freedom vs. Naïve Freewill Thinking* article accessed on April 19, 2011 at http://www.egodeath.com/TranscendingDeterminismVsNaiveFreewill.htm

Interestingly, most philosophers believe the ego to be an inhabitant, as it were, of one's consciousness.

It becomes in transcending the ego that one is able to experience [1] increased rest and relaxation (from the questioning, analysing, judging and scheming of the ego), [2] increased inner knowing (gnosis), [3] an enhanced sense of oneness with all creation, [4] increased creativity, stillness and clarity, and [5] a sense of liberation (from conflict and stress as well as from a sense of needing to defend the ego). [144]

The Bhagavad-Gita (the eternal message of spiritual wisdom from ancient India) talks about transcending the ego. The word Gita means song and the word Bhagavad means God; often the Bhagavad-Gita is called the Song of God.

One can locate the Bhagavad-Gita in the historical epic Mahabharata (as written by Vedavyasa), which contains the essence of the Vedas.

---

[144] *Transcending the Ego: Healing Egocentricity via Soul Connection* article accessed on April 20, 2011 at http://www.brothermichael.org.uk/resources/soul.htm

It is said that in studying the <u>Bhagavad-Gita</u>, one will gain "accurate, fundamental knowledge about God, the ultimate truth, creation, birth and death, the results of actions, the eternal soul, liberation and the purpose as well as the goal of human existence." [145]

Those that teach enlightenment (based on the information that stems from India and which also includes the <u>Bhagavad-Gita</u>) all agree on one issue: transcending the ego. In wanting to advance on a spiritual level, this is something that must be accomplished.

The ego exists in the form of emotions, feelings, beliefs and desires. To transcend the ego does not mean that we get rid of it; it simply means that you must learn to recognize it for what it is: an illusion (of separation) to which all are attached.

It is the knowing, believing and accepting that you are no different from anyone else, because everything exists in the oneness of creation (which means that you fully

---

[145] http://www.bhagavad-gita.org/Articles/faq.html

acknowledge and recognize that you are something much greater than the egoic self) that allows you to begin the process of transcending the ego.

Free from both prejudice and judgment, you experience a deep sense of complete freedom.

You are not here to destroy the ego.

You are not here to dissolve the ego.

You are not here to kill the ego.

You are here to learn to become the detached observer.

You are also here to still the chatter of your mind.

You are here to transcend the ego, which has a need to protect, defend and secure your physical identity (social status, reputation (which sometimes also translates as having power over other people), nationality, religion, closed belief systems), so that both mind and spirit (heart) can merge together, thereby working in unison.

We need "to be aware of our individual identities while simultaneously developing an expanded sense of global consciousness. Then we need to make sure both of these levels of awareness are aligned." [146]

The realization that you are more than just your ego (emotions, feelings, beliefs, desires, life experiences) is what allows you to begin to engage the world more fully, more completely, more consciously.

It becomes in recognizing the fact that thoughts and behaviors at the individual (personal) level also impact thoughts and behaviors at the global (collective) level, that you will have successfully transformed (transcended) the ego. This is the very level from which you must begin this expansive work.

As you come to realize that you are part of the macrocosm (the bigger picture, the same stream of consciousness to which all are connected), you will have reconciled yourself with the knowingness that "if you can live constructively as

---

[146] *The War on Ego* article accessed on April 20, 2011 at
http://www.stevepavlina.com/blog/2008/03/the-war-on-ego/

an individual, and if you can influence enough of the other cells to make similar changes, you'll have a positive impact on shifting the larger body [of humanity] to more constructive behaviors." [147]

When I continue to align my choices with the higher good, knowing and believing that my choices are also serving to help others, I feel as if I am mysteriously guided and directed to the right circumstances, the right people, and the right situations. This is what happens when I am writing.

It must also be remembered that when I help another, I am also helping myself.

In short, achieving global consciousness, one individual at a time, is what lies at the crux of this undertaking.

The main caution is that "you have to stay focused on the overlap between your individual good and the good of humanity. This takes a bit of practice because it's a different way of thinking about life than most people are

---

[147] *The War on Ego* article accessed on April 20, 2011 at
http://www.stevepavlina.com/blog/2008/03/the-war-on-ego/

taught. We're encouraged to think about how our actions affect the people closest to us, but not the entire body of humanity. There is an effect though, and it does make a difference." [148]

Transcendence resides within.

The spirit that exists within is both formless and eternal.

It becomes in acknowledging and living this knowledge that the ego loses its power.

Seeking and claiming the power within is the only way to transcend.

It was Isaac the Syrian who explained the purpose of silence as awakening the mind to God. [149]

It is author David Darling who refers to the pivotal moment in awakening as being the switchover from "normal

---

[148] *The War on Ego* article accessed on April 20, 2011 at
http://www.stevepavlina.com/blog/2008/03/the-war-on-ego/
[149] http://www.theosophical.org/publications/quest-magazine/1432

dualistic mode of thinking to the selfless experience of transcendence." [150]

Known by a multitude of different names (satori, nirvana, Tao, enlightenment, zoning, bliss), this fundamental mystical feeling, also called *The Perennial Philosophy*, may come "after years of asceticism, study, and devotion to some particular religious or meditation system." [151]

Likewise, for most ordinary folk, it may arrive "out of the blue, unbidden and unsought" [152] given that "the very act of seeking may block or hinder the experience of enlightenment." [153]

The feeling of transcendent unity "is the same for everyone when it happens, since there is only one reality. However, problems ensue in translating this feeling into words. Even greater difficulties arise when others, who have not had the

---

[150]

http://www.daviddarling.info/works/ZenPhysics/ZenPhysics_ch13.html
[151] Ibid.
[152] Ibid.
[153] Ibid.

experience themselves, try to convey, second hand or third hand, what the fundamental teaching consisted of." [154]

Once again ... *to know something, you must become it.*

From the reasonably clear and simple message of Gautama Buddha, "the vast and intricate system of religious philosophy that is Buddhism has sprung. Thousands of books and many millions of words have been set down on the subject, often in a style that only a lifetime devotee or learned academic could penetrate, but the irony is that language and symbolism are anathema to the basic message of Buddha, which is all about *direct experience and unadulterated being.* And the same is true of Christianity. The central teaching of Jesus, a flesh-and-blood human being like you and me, was to *forget yourself and get in touch with the real world.*" [155]

---

[154]

http://www.daviddarling.info/works/ZenPhysics/ZenPhysics_ch13.html
[155] Ibid.

Mind you, there can be "no proof of transcendence without the necessary self-transformation. Adopting an attitude of humility, and recognizing one's lack of knowledge, in order to seriously consider a transcendental philosophy, can be a beneficial exercise in and of itself." [156]

In the words of Albert Einstein ... *there are moments when one feels free from one's own identification with human limitations and inadequacies. At such moments, one imagines that one stands on some spot of a small planet, gazing in amazement at the cold yet profoundly moving beauty of the eternal, the unfathomable: life and death flow into one, and there is neither evolution nor destiny; only being.*

Clearly, this was an individual who understood his purpose, both as a scientist as well as a human being. Ultimately, what needs to be transcended are the limiting beliefs, the ignorance, the victim consciousness and the anger, all of which hold us back from our true selves.

---

[156] *Transition to Transcendence* article accessed on April 23, 2011 at http://www.cejournal.org/GRD/Wolff.htm

Once your consciousness transcends "into quantum realms, you will not be above others or better than others, but you will be much more present in the here and now, channelling into space/time the grace of your higher consciousness." [157]

It was also Albert Einstein who said ... *The intuitive mind is a sacred gift and the rational mind is a faithful servant. We have created a society that honours the servant and has forgotten the gift.*

There is no better time, than now, to both acknowledge and embrace this outstanding gift. In fact, the road to transcendence can only be traveled by way of intuitive (or nonlinear) thinking.

It is deep contemplation and introspection (focusing inward) that will enable you to become more intuitive. So, too, must you learn to discern the difference between genuine intuition and subjective bias.

---

[157] *Becoming Galactic: Presuppositions of Quantum Consciousness* blog article accessed on April 23, 2011 at http://www.becoming-galactic.org/presupp8.html

For example, "if an idea feels off, then find out exactly why it feels off. If an idea feels right, then find out exactly why. You are not finished until you clearly understand the intuitive impression, have logically dissected it, and can convey it accurately in words. Doing so is a divine act because it gives clear voice to spirit. It is really an internal communion, a nonverbal socratic dialogue between the lower self and the higher Self. You turn within, pose the question, feel out the possibilities, investigate the results, correct misunderstandings, apply them, test them, revise them, learn from them, ask and receive, feel out and figure out, realize and transcend." [158]

If your intuition is correct, then, it becomes "in following and testing it [that] you will encounter new observations, new experiences, and revised assumptions that prove it. Since intuition comes from beyond, the proof of its validity is accessed by going beyond." [159]

---

[158] *Transcendence Through Intuitive Thinking* article accessed on July 28, 2011 at http://montalk.net/metaphys/138/transcendence-through-intuitive-thinking
[159] Ibid.

This, then, is what constitutes "the true scientific method, where a hypothesis is proposed first and then tested. Too many scientists and skeptics irrationally reject "far out" hypotheses before investigating them solely because these "wild assertions" are not yet supported by prevailing assumptions. They are afraid to take a single step without the certainty of group consensus and the absolute confirmation of all prior steps, and so they are barred from accessing higher levels of objectivity and instead rationalize away transjective influences. Intuitive thinking is more scientific than modern science because it does not allow the scientific method to be restrained by limitations irrationally imposed by old assumptions. It is the way of the gnostic intellectual rather than the agnostic rationalist. *Intuitive thinking is the true science of transcendence.*" [160]

Intuitive thinking also leads you to the truth(s) that exist within; the truth(s) that resonate with you.

---

[160] *Transcendence Through Intuitive Thinking* article accessed on July 28, 2011 at http://montalk.net/metaphys/138/transcendence-through-intuitive-thinking

As you are constantly evolving and growing, so, too, is it with the truth(s) that you hold.

Enlightenment is a state of being whereby you are reunited with your true spiritual self.

Indeed, this is what is meant by the words Holy Grail.

For the most part, antagonism refers to a *form of hostility* that generally results in active resistance, opposition, or contentiousness (which may also result in animosity, bitterness, argumentativeness, belligerence as well as aggressiveness).

Antagonism is directly related to conditioning and fear, so you may wish to revisit these particular chapters.

Antagonism is also what can lead to both destructive conflict as well as war, amidst the collision of core moral values, which, in turn, becomes the right versus right argument.

It becomes in understanding the value differences that "we can easily see why we have a conflict: each value is right by one perspective, and each appears to exclude the other." [161]

---

[161] *Dealing with Antagonists* article accessed on July 28, 2011 at http://www.essentialism.net/antagonists.htm

Merely attempting to analyze the dilemma does not even come close to resolving the situation. Resolution "requires us to choose which side is the *nearest* right for the circumstances." [162]

There exist three possible means with which to think through right versus right issues; namely, [1] ends-based thinking (best known by the maxim ... *do whatever produces the greatest good for the greatest number*); [2] rule-based thinking (which is often associated with the 18th century German philosopher, Immanuel Kant, whose words today simply translate to *follow only the principle that you want everyone else to follow*) and [3] care-based thinking (which frequently employs the Golden Rule argument, in that you *do unto others what you would like them to do unto you*). [163]

Unfortunately, it is the employ of antagonism that always leads to greater conflict.

Antagonism involves resistance and fighting.

---

[162] *Dealing with Antagonists* article accessed on July 28, 2011 at http://www.essentialism.net/antagonists.htm
[163] Ibid.

Life does not have to be conquered, despite the fact that this is what has been taught, and lived, for thousands of years.

When you continue to live life in this manner, you are the prime loser for you have separated yourself from the inherent goodness and wholesomeness of life.

You simply have to come to the realization that you are an important part of that which constitutes the totality of life.

In realizing that you are part of the macrocosm (the bigger picture, the same stream of consciousness to which all are connected), in truth, is there any point to fighting with yourself?

Nothing is more valuable than life.

Nothing is more valuable than taking the time to experience each moment in its divine radiance, which means that one must be willing to take the risk of being in love with life, of being in love with creation, of being in love with who you are; in essence, of being in love with existence.

As Osho shares ... *Love is the ultimate need. Everything else is secondary. Everything else is just a means to that great end. If love happens, then all has happened; if love does not happen, then nothing has happened and the whole of life has just been a wasteland.* [164]

Love is the only true answer that exists for every question that will ever be asked.

---

[164] http://www.oshoteachings.com/osho-take-the-risk-of-being-in-love-with-existence/

# *Empowerment*

Empowerment is a process whereby individuals and groups are able to make choices (be they spiritual, political, social, economic, workplace or gender related), based on accessible information, and then transforming those choices into desired actions (and, hence, desired outcomes).

As a result, empowerment is also synonymous with the ability to reclaim one's power.

Empowerment, then, becomes *knowing what you want* and *knowing what you do not want*.

It becomes in being able to express knowledge and understanding from both camps, clearly, succinctly and calmly (without engaging any degree of emotional attachment), that you are able to detach from the outcome in a secure, loving and compassionate manner.

One who is truly empowered "would never interfere with another; one who is truly empowered would never seek to control another or impose his or her will upon another; one

who is truly empowered would never judge another." [165]
This serves to constitute spiritual empowerment; the key to
remembering the sacredness of all life.

The state that "you are in at any given time is completely up
to you. We create our state of mind, relative to the state of
our conscious awareness. The more conscious you become
of how the vehicle of your body and mind work, the more
control you will have over your senses and your life." [166]

The operative terms here are *the more conscious you become*
which is really what this existence is all about. Being
spiritually empowered means that you have taken back your
personal power, meaning that you are now able to take
charge of what you do, what you think, what you feel, and
how you respond to whatever comes into your life.

Ultimately, spiritual empowerment means that you take
conscious control of everything that matters to you.

---

[165] Manifest Messenger email series (as taken from *Journey Into Now*
by Leonard Jacobson) received from Jackie Lapin on June 23, 2011.
[166] Manifest Messenger email series (as taken from *The Awakening* by
Steven S. Sadleir) received from Jackie Lapin on June 14, 2011.

To free yourself from entanglement on all levels, "you will have to bring to consciousness all the ways that you lose yourself in others. Each time you notice that you are seeking love, acceptance, or approval from another, you will have to own, acknowledge, and confess that you are giving away your power. If you are trying to please another to gain acceptance, [you must] own, acknowledge, and confess it without judgment." [167]

Spiritual empowerment begins with the realization that you are a spiritual being having a physical experience; that you are here to experience yourself in all ways. It becomes this very belief that lends itself to the next phase, whereby you come to the realization that it is through the power of your mind (through the reconfiguring of your subconscious as well as the redirecting of your conscious awareness) that you are able to create the world that you wish to create for yourself.

Ultimately, the choice rests with you.

---

[167] Manifest Messenger email series (as taken from *Journey Into Now* by Leonard Jacobson) received from Jackie Lapin on June 27, 2011.

As you awaken to your divine and infinite essence, you begin to live the qualities of love, respect, compassion, empathy and nonjudgment.

In knowing that you are everything and everything is you; in knowing that God is present in every thought, every word, every emotion, every action, and every deed, this is what further propels you to begin living a more conscious existence.

By direct association, the practices of meditation, prayer and contemplation become even more meaningful (insightful), further enabling you to discern that which ultimately is your truth.

Every thought, every word, every emotion, every action, and every deed is the result of either positive or negative thinking.

It is only "through awareness of, and creatively working with, our thoughts, feelings and emotions that we manifest more positive qualities within. Through being increasingly aware of our actions and reactions, we become more spiritually responsible. Until we have awakened to self-awareness, we can never truly know who we are and fully trust ourselves. We see that self-awareness is not just about spiritual and psychic development, but the whole of what we are." [168]

Likewise, by "being aware of how we act in everyday life, we can grow into more centred and loving individuals, and by cultivating our minds and looking after our bodies, become more active forces for good. All are part of the process of discovering who we really are, and can be used as vehicles for transformation and expressing the true Self. With spiritual gifts, the more open and cultivated the mind is, the more receptive the individual will be to higher and refined influences." [169]

Knowing that we are an integral part of God, so, too, is everything derived from God.

---

[168] Edwards, Gly and Santoshan. *Steps to Spiritual Empowerment* article accessed on July 30, 2011 at
http://www.spiritualistresources.com/cgi-bin/articles/index.pl?read=40
[169] Ibid.

All creative potentials and possibilities "are within this spirit that we are. We need to recognise that it is through our minds, emotions and individuality, that we develop the ability to be more Divinity-centred, and establish greater awareness of who we are and how we interconnect with all life. The more we are able to recognise this reality, the more receptive we will be to infinite qualities of good within us. This will give us the strength to free the mind and emotions, and embrace a greater Truth." [170]

As you seek to understand the purpose of life, you learn that peace, joy and harmony reign supreme when you choose to live life from a higher spiritual viewpoint (embracing the essence, the totality, of who you are).

All of life is interconnected, in ways that we cannot even begin to fathom.

Knowing that we have "within us infinite qualities of good, love and compassion ... every act, thought and expression

---

[170] Edwards, Gly and Santoshan. *Steps to Spiritual Empowerment* article accessed on July 30, 2011 at
http://www.spiritualistresources.com/cgi-bin/articles/index.pl?read=40

can be reflected upon and used to unfold these qualities more purely. By doing this, we make our lives a constant meditation and uncover a sense of the inherent universal Self in everyday life; we become less self-centred and more in tune with life and our spirit." [171]

All of life is sacred. Knowing and believing this to be true, we should "seek to become one with this sacredness that exists in everything and everyone, and respect and care for all life, including ourselves. Anything that separates us from others means separating ourselves from life and the creative Principle in all." [172]

Living by spiritual law means "taking responsibility for every area of our lives – our thoughts, our feelings, our actions – and being respectful of everyone and every form of life we come into contact with … [in order to] become more caring, loving, centred and responsible human beings." [173]

---

[171] Edwards, Gly and Santoshan. *Steps to Spiritual Empowerment* article accessed on July 30, 2011 at http://www.spiritualistresources.com/cgi-bin/articles/index.pl?read=40
[172] Ibid.
[173] Ibid.

Respect also means coming to understand that you can only change yourself.

Respect also means that you must allow another to work their way through their own experiences.

There will always be times when you find that you are unable to do something physically about a given situation. This is when you may only be able to work on the metaphysical level, assisting in other ways. For example, "by discovering your inner truth, manifesting it as practical knowledge, and maintaining your frequency and confidence in what you know, you become a beacon broadcasting higher frequency and higher knowledge into your environment and into the lives of all who cross your path. You create ripple effects in reality, sending waves out through the lives of others. You throw seeds and they grow in those whose minds are fertile. You create a forward cascading effect into the future, in ways only the divine mind can grasp in its entirety because the future is nonlinear; small things can have HUGE effects if applied in the right way at the right place at the right time. It's not about "right" and "wrong" but a matter of what needs to be done and the wisest way of doing it." [174]

This is what constitutes spiritual empowerment.

---

[174] *Maximizing Your Potential to Help Others* article accessed on July 30, 2011 at http://montalk.net/metaphys/59/maximizing-your-potential-to-help-others

If we have a negative thought "it reduces the vibratory frequency of our cells and we become more susceptible [to illness and disease]. If we are angry or critical, our cells vibrate at a slower pace and we can become ill." [175]

If we truly believe, as I do, "that in our unity with our brothers and sisters of the one humanity, we know that we affect each other just as the butterfly affects the whole world with the flutter of its wings," [176] then there are things that each can do, in turn, to raise the vibratory frequency of their cells, such as ......

[1] meditating, [2] transcending critical (judgmental) thoughts of self and others, [3] choosing to speak with words that heal, [4] transcending all boundaries (political, social, religious, gender, racial), [5] blessing everyone who crosses

---

[175] Vernon, Rama Jyoti. *Japan, Radiation and Spiritual Emergence* article accessed on June 28, 2011 at
http://www.ramavernon.com/Radiation.html
[176] Ibid.

your path [6] remembering that you share a Oneness with everyone and everything, [7] displaying the ability to forgive, [8] surrounding yourself with plants, crystals and salt lamps (in order to create a healing atmosphere that will serve to produce an abundance of negative ions), [9] turning off non-ionizing radiation equipment at night (computers, televisions and cell phones), [10] luxuriating in Epsom salt baths, [11] reducing sugar intake (which also includes high sugar vegetables and fruit), [12] eating foods that are high in antioxidants, [13] eating alkalizing food, [14] eating foods that are low on the food chain, and [15] taking more time to relax (which serves to boost the immune system and keep one healthy). [177]

In doing your best to remain positive and upbeat, there are many components that need to be fine tuned (limiting thought patterns, negative emotions, underlying feelings of anxiety and stress), otherwise they shall continue to get in the way of that which you desire to create for yourself.

---

[177] Vernon, Rama Jyoti. *Japan, Radiation and Spiritual Emergence* article accessed on June 28, 2011 at
http://www.ramavernon.com/Radiation.html

Tensions come from a block, or imbalance, in a flow of energy within us. "When we hold onto the feelings that are moving through us, the pent up energy creates blockages and imbalances that result in tension and pain. When we allow a feeling, as energy in our body, to flow naturally through us without resistance from holding onto the feeling by identifying with it, then we can move with that energy and allow it to guide us through our life experience." [178]

The more positive you are, the happier your life becomes. In fact, it is through the power of positive thinking that you can change your life.

Positive thinking is a mental attitude that you develop, that you cultivate, that you become determined to live by.

In short, positive thinking is a mindset that is "conductive to growth, expansion and success. It is a mental attitude that expects good and favorable results ... [because] a positive

---

[178] Manifest Messenger email series (as taken from *The Awakening* by Steven S. Sadleir) received from Jackie Lapin on June 17, 2011.

mind anticipates happiness, joy, health and a successful outcome of every situation and action." [179]

By comparison, "negative thoughts, words and attitude bring up negative and unhappy moods and actions. When the mind is negative, poisons are released into the blood, which cause more unhappiness and negativity ... [leading] the way to failure, frustration and disappointment." [180]

To develop a more positive mindset, much inner work and training is required. As most can attest, your attitudes and thoughts do not change overnight.

Not wanting to dissuade you in any way, I have to share that this is a process that can, and often does, take several years.

I know because I have lived the process; likewise, I am continuing to do so.

---

[179] Sasson, Remez. *The Power of Positive Thinking* article accessed on July 30, 2011 at
http://www.successconsciousness.com/index_000009.htm
[180] Ibid.

First off, it becomes imperative that you take the time to read more about this subject (by going to Goggle and offering terms such as: positive thinking, positive attitude, positive mindset, the power of the mind, will power, self discipline, the power of concentration, motivation, the law of attraction, affirmations, creative visualization, meditation, happiness, peace of mind, nonduality, spiritual growth).

As you are researching, you also need to take the time to think about all of the benefits that are to be gleaned from wholeheartedly embracing such an approach.

The power of thought is what shapes our lives. While most of this shaping is usually done subconsciously, you can make the process a conscious one.

You may need to "ignore what others might say or think about you, if they discover that you are changing the way you think." [181]

---

[181] Sasson, Remez. *The Power of Positive Thinking* article accessed on July 30, 2011 at
http://www.successconsciousness.com/index_000009.htm

Part of the process involves always visualizing "only favorable and beneficial situations. Use positive words in your inner dialogues or when talking with others. Smile a little more, as this helps to think positively. Disregard any feelings of laziness or a desire to quit … [because] if you persevere, you will transform the way your mind thinks." [182]

As soon as a negative thought enters your mind, you must learn to become aware of it, endeavouring to replace it with a more constructive one.

You must also become aware that the negative thought will try, countless times, to enter your mind; it becomes your job, each time thereafter, to replace it with a positive one.

It is persistence that will "eventually teach your mind to think positively and ignore negative thoughts." [183]

---

[182] Sasson, Remez. *The Power of Positive Thinking* article accessed on July 30, 2011 at
http://www.successconsciousness.com/index_000009.htm
[183] Ibid.

Please believe me when I tell you that the power exists within for you to be successful, in this endeavour, should that be your choice.

Thinking positive thoughts, reciting personally tailored affirmations, and utilizing creative visualization, all the while expecting only favourable results, are what will pave the way to change in situations as well as circumstances.

The Silk Routes (collectively known as the Silk Road) were important paths for cultural and commercial exchange between traders, merchants, pilgrims, missionaries, soldiers, nomads and urban dwellers from Ancient China, Ancient India, Ancient Tibet, the Persian (Parthian) Empire and Mediterranean countries for close to 3,000 years.

Receiving its name from the lucrative Chinese silk trade, this was the major reason for turning the connection of trade routes into an extensive trans-continental network.

The Old Silk Road has many tales to share with us, one being The Lost Sutras of Jesus.

The Emperor, Taizong, "envisioned China as the civilizing center of the world. He granted foreigners the rights and privileges of Chinese citizens," [184] welcoming those with

---

[184] Riegert, Ray and Moore, Thomas; editors. (2003) *The Lost Sutras of Jesus: Unlocking the Ancient Wisdom of the Xian Monks* (page 7). Berkeley, CA: Seastone.

beliefs alien to the Tang Dynasty. As a result, Monks from across Asia "were soon teaching in Xian and Chinese pilgrims set out for India to collect Buddhist scriptures." [185]

In 635 AD (the seventh century), Aleben, a Nestorian bishop from Persia, along with his followers, journeyed 3,000 miles along the Old Silk Road, to the Chinese Imperial city Chang-an (today known as Xian).

The text he carried "told of a savior who would free humankind." [186] It was not long thereafter that the monks were busy "rendering their sacred texts into Chinese characters." [187]

As Persian Christians, "Aleben and his band believed Mary was the mother of Jesus the man, not the god. They were captivated by the historical Jesus and treated his teachings like those of a sage." [188] While the Jesus Sutras do not carry

---

[185] Riegert, Ray and Moore, Thomas; editors. (2003) *The Lost Sutras of Jesus: Unlocking the Ancient Wisdom of the Xian Monks* (page 7). Berkeley, CA: Seastone.
[186] Ibid.
[187] Ibid, page 8.
[188] Ibid, page 13.

canon status, they clearly merge Christian philosophy with both Buddhist and Taoist thought.

The original documents, theorized by historians to have been written in Syriac (a language that would have been closely related to the native tongue of Jesus), have never been found; instead, "only ancient scrolls containing the Chinese translations remain." [189]

The Jesus of the Gospels "teaches a life of peace, humility, paradox and egolessness. It's a short step [thereafter] to the Asian concepts of action through non-action and compassion through transcendence of the self. By taking Buddhist and Taoist teachings on yin and yang, the eternal law within things, and the search for an end to manic activity, and then combining them with the parables of Jesus, the Sutras create a more complex and deeply visionary form of Christianity." [190]

---

[189] Riegert, Ray and Moore, Thomas; editors. (2003) *The Lost Sutras of Jesus: Unlocking the Ancient Wisdom of the Xian Monks* (page 9). Berkeley, CA: Seastone.
[190] Ibid, page 124.

The Church of the East broke away from the West just in time, then, to avoid both "the magnificence and the curse of St. Augustine of Hippo, who took the basic notion of original sin and built it into the destructive force it was to become. In looking at the theology of the Church of the East, we can see what Christianity without St. Augustine might have been like." [191]

It was St. Augustine who saw "humanity as almost irredeemably wicked and perverse, rejecting any idea of some innate goodness. Augustine was opposed in his time by the first British theologian, on record, a monk named Pelagius, who argued the opposite: that human nature was basically good but had been corrupted and misguided by human weakness. The theology of Augustine triumphed in the West, but it was a theology similar to Pelagius's, that triumphed in China." [192]

---

[191] Palmer, Martin. *Original Nature Not Original Sin: Extract from The Jesus Sutras* article accessed on March 26, 2011 at http://www.goldenageproject.org.uk/968.php
[192] Ibid.

The term *original nature* or *innate nature* occurs in both Taoist and Buddhist thought, signifying "that all life is innately good but becomes corrupt, or loses its way, through the compromises of life and existence." [193]

In these Christian Sutras from China "is the shape or outline of a post-Augustinian theology that the West itself needs in order to become free from the burden of original sin and thus reconfigure or rediscover Christianity. Given that original sin was unknown as a central theme of Christian thought before the early fifth century, it is possible to agree with Pelagius that true Christianity holds a notion of original goodness. In a post Augustinian Christian world, this rediscovery, embodied in the actual books and thoughts of a major ancient Church, may well be a version of Christianity that can speak to spiritual seekers today." [194]

---

[193] Palmer, Martin. *Original Nature Not Original Sin: Extract from The Jesus Sutras* article accessed on March 26, 2011 at http://www.goldenageproject.org.uk/968.php
[194] Ibid.

Given that Buddhism was practiced throughout the Persian (Parthian) Empire, many living in Jerusalem, during the time of Jesus, would have had some familiarity with this religion.

In fact, "Buddhism was practiced throughout the Parthian empire during those years and even began its spread to China through missionaries from Parthia beginning only a mere century before Jesus' birth. The borders of the Parthian empire spread all the way to Roman-occupied Jerusalem from India, where Buddhism began." [195]

Healers were "not so uncommon in Buddhism, but in Jerusalem they were mostly unheard of. Anyone with such abilities would have been seen as a prophet of God by many Jews, regardless of the source of their healing powers; others would have seen him as a devil. Such was the way in which Jesus was received." [196]

---

[195] Madsen, Isaac T. (2008) *Comparison Between Jesus and Buddha* article accessed on March 23, 2011 at http://www.helium.com/items/1079256-jesus-and-buddhahttpwwwheliumcomitems1079256-jesus-and-buddhaedit
[196] Ibid.

The 27 books of the New Testament constitute the fundamental holy scripture of Christianity.

Without the four Gospels according to Matthew, Mark, Luke and John, "Christianity is virtually null and void. Recent epoch-making discoveries of old Sanskrit manuscripts in Central Asia and Kashmir provide decisive proof that *the four Greek Gospels have been translated directly from the Sanskrit.* A careful comparison, word by word, sentence by sentence, shows that the Christian Gospels are Pirate-copies of the Buddhist Gospels (combined, of course, with words from the OT). God's word, therefore, is originally Buddha's word." [197]

Christian Lindtner, of Denmark, states that the best way to engage in a serious study of the four New Testament Gospels "is to start by counting the number of verses, the

---

[197] Lindtner, Christian. *Jesus Is Buddha* website accessed on March 23, 2011 at http://www.jesusisbuddha.com/

number of words, the number of syllables and the number of letters that the Greek text, of course, consists of." [198]

While this might appear an unreasonable place to begin, he shares that in so doing, "you will soon see that the unknown authors of the Gospels must have paid extreme attention to each word and syllable, to their number and to their numerical value, what the Greeks call psêphos." [199]

In keeping, the authors of the New Testament also "paid great attention to the size of syllables, words and sentences. The technical term for this phenomenon is gematria, from the Hebrew gymtry, which, again, is from the Greek geômetría (first attested in Herodotus)." [200]

---

[198] Lindtner, Christian. (2003) *The Christian Lindtner Theory (CLR) of the Buddhist Origins of the New Testament Gospels* article accessed on March 23, 2011 at http://www.jesusisbuddha.com/CLT.html
[199] Ibid.
[200] Ibid.

One could then say that the Gospels, "at least to some extent, report geometrical figures, rather than historical facts." [201]

The Christian Lindtner Theory (CLT) briefly states that the Gospels, "perhaps even the New Testament books as a whole, are a Pirate-copy of the Buddhist Gospels, or of the Buddha's Testament." [202]

In speaking of pirate copies, he means that the Gospels "not only imitate the sense of the Sanskrit originals" [203] but so, too, do the Gospels "also imitate the form and the numerical values found at various levels in the original." [204]

Lindtner believes the Q Gospel (on which Matthew, Mark and Luke are said to be have been based) was a combination of several Buddhist Sanskrit texts; namely, the Mûlasarvâstivâdavinaya [abbreviated as MSV] and the

---

[201] Lindtner, Christian. (2003) *The Christian Lindtner Theory (CLR) of the Buddhist Origins of the New Testament Gospels* article accessed on March 23, 2011 at http://www.jesusisbuddha.com/CLT.html
[202] Ibid.
[203] Ibid.
[204] Ibid.

Saddharmapundarîka [abbreviated as SDP], saying that scholars have "failed to identify Q simply because they did not consider reading MSV and SDP in the original Sanskrit," [205] meaning that any serious comparison between the life and teachings of Buddha and Jesus "must start out by carefully comparing the original Greek and the Sanskrit texts." [206]

Both Buddha and Jesus taught compassion, selflessness and intolerance.

As historical characters, both Jesus and Buddha are worth recognizing.

Might there be a possibility that a connection exists between the two?

---

[205] Lindtner, Christian. (2003) *The Christian Lindtner Theory (CLR) of the Buddhist Origins of the New Testament Gospels* article accessed on March 23, 2011 at http://www.jesusisbuddha.com/CLT.html
[206] Lindtner, Christian. (May 2003) Book Review article accessed on March 23, 2011 at http://www.jesusisbuddha.com/lebenundlehre.html

Interesting comparisons are denoted in the research conducted by Suzanne Olsson, author of <u>Jesus in Kashmir: The Lost Tomb</u>, especially when she states that "the word Sakya is believed by many scholars to derive from the name Isaac ... and is directly linked with Gautama Buddha's family name, which is Shakya, Sakymanu or Shakimuni," [207] meaning that if these Sakyas are descendants of Isaac, then so, too, was Gautama Buddha a descendant of Isaac.

Could it be, then, that Buddha may have had Jewish grandfathers in the same lineage as Jesus? I see this as being something that merits further investigation.

Is it possible that such an exploration might well demonstrate the oneness of *all* world religions, thereby connecting the bloodlines of *all* peoples?

Perhaps therein lies the true vision for all.

---

[207] Olsson, Suzanne. (2005) *Jesus in Kashmir: The Lost Tomb* (page 31). Charleston, SC: Booksurge.

---

Dharma, a Sanskrit word that means Law or Natural Law, also translates as *spiritual reality*.

In that stead, I see dharma as living in a manner appropriate to universal truth (meaning justice, social harmony and human happiness); after all, true spirituality must be experiential.

Dharma, then, is "not something that is alien to our normal human experience. This Spiritual Realm (Dharma Dhatu) is the reality of one's very own mind. It is also the mind of the Buddha and the mind of all living beings," [208] therein denoting the interconnectedness of all life.

Dharma is not a religion, it is not a teaching, nor is it something that is separate from the soul.

---

[208] *Dharma Spirituality* article accessed on July 30, 2011 at
http://www.tientai.net/teachings/dharma/6realms/fa1.htm

Dharma can also be translated as *one's duty towards others* as well as *one's duty towards the self* (in realizing the inherent truth that resides within). [209]

In effect, everything that makes you who you are can also be considered dharma, meaning that if you are following your dharma, your truth, you will not fail. [210]

We are a melding of *God-man* (the mind of God expressing in human form) and *man-God* (physical man expressing the God within), a combined merger of spiritual and physical that serves to continue the expansion of the Father into forever.

However, instead of focusing on the God that resides outside of the self, and has become religion, we are here to learn to focus on the God that resides within, that which becomes one's spirituality.

---

[209] *Dharma Spirituality* article accessed on July 30, 2011 at http://www.tientai.net/teachings/dharma/6realms/fa1.htm
[210] http://video.ezinemark.com/dharma-spirituality-enlightenment-spiritual-path-person-4729c4f88ac.html

Spiritual maturity "can be described in many ways. The Map of Consciousness, [located within *Power vs. Force: The Hidden Determinants of Human Behavior*] by Dr. David R. Hawkins, is very illuminating ... and very helpful in understanding the wide variety of levels of consciousness we see being expressed. Basically, being spiritually mature involves awareness, love and integrity." [211]

Dharma, then, can be seen as a living path to God realization.

---

[211] Sanders, Egan. *Spiritual Maturity: Spirituality and Sensibility* article accessed on July 30, 2011 at
http://www.egansanders.com/archives/spiritual_maturity.html

Utopia has been defined as [1] *any real or imaginary place or state (society) considered to be perfect or ideal* as well as [2] *any visionary system of political or social perfection.*

Change is the only constant. The questions that bode asking then become … "What can you do in this moment? What is there to enjoy in your current experience?" [212]

Utopia may not, in actual fact, "be a destination, but simply enjoyable moments along the way, " [213] thereby making it a spiritual place as opposed to an actual physical place or space.

Knowing that you are what you live inside, can it not also be said that you can live your own Utopian-based existence, the province of your own truth-filled heart and soul, so to speak?

---

[212] Sanders, Egan. *Spiritual Maturity: Spirituality and Sensibility* article accessed on July 30, 2011 at
http://www.egansanders.com/archives/spiritual_maturity.html
[213] Ibid.

What might be the pertinent steps, if any, to getting there?

[1] desire for a change

[2] an increase in consciousness

[3] becoming that which you seek (love, peace, forgiveness, unity, altruism, tranquility, freedom)

[4] living that which you seek

[5] following the dictates of your heart

[6] living a heart-based consciousness

[7] demonstrating unconditional love for all life

At present, the Findhorn Foundation Community, located in northeast Scotland, on the Moray Firth coast, may well be the closest model we have to the Utopian-based spiritual community. Theirs is a "spiritual community, ecovillage and an international centre for holistic education, helping to unfold a new human consciousness and create a positive and sustainable future." [214]

---

[214] http://www.findhorn.org/aboutus/vision/

You should *always* follow your heart, doing that which you feel inspired to do.

On a practical basis this "could be sharing with needy individuals and local charitable groups whatever resources you have (time, talents and skills, knowledge, money, tools and equipment, transportation, shelter) or supporting national and international organizations engaged in environmental preservation or legal, political and economic reforms." [215]

On a spiritual basis this could simply mean visualizing "the world you want for yourselves, your children and their children: a world of love, peace, mutual respect and life in harmony with all of Nature" [216] because one should never

---

[215] Beckow, Steve. (2011) *Background and Analysis of Matthew's June 11, 2011 Message* article accessed on June 12, 2011 at http://stevebeckow.com/2011/06/background-and-analysis-of-matthews-june-11-2011-message/
[216] Ibid

underestimate their "power to turn visions and thoughts into actuality." [217]

In essence, you are ultimately the master of your own inner world.

In the words of Earl Nightingale … *We can let circumstances rule us, or we can take charge and rule our lives from within.*

Passion is defined as [1] *any powerful or compelling emotion or feeling,* [2] *a strong or extravagant enthusiasm or desire for something,* [3] *an outburst of strong emotion or feeling.*

We all have a passion.

When you love what you do, so completely and thoroughly, you are at one with your Higher Self, with your divine essence.

---

[217] Beckow, Steve. (2011) *Background and Analysis of Matthew's June 11, 2011 Message* article accessed on June 12, 2011 at http://stevebeckow.com/2011/06/background-and-analysis-of-matthews-june-11-2011-message/

When you fall in love with an idea to the point whereby it has become your passion, the divine is expressing through you.

When you love what you do, so completely and thoroughly, you are creating for yourself.

The most truly amazing thing is that you are also creating for others because this burning desire, as felt by you, can only serve to benefit another.

Locating your passion, demonstrating persistence and the will to achieve, and taking action while refusing to give up: *these are the very attributes* that will allow you to achieve that which you desire.

Find what it is that you love. Find what it is that gives you joy. Find what it is that gives your life meaning.

You will know when you have found your passion, your bliss, your burning desire.

Do not settle for anything less.

Do what you love and you will love what you do.

Let this be the very inspiration that you choose to live by.

Authenticity can be likened to spiritual archaeology, as in digging with your soul, with your heart, with your spirit, searching for something that fulfills the real you. [218]

In the course of my research on authenticity, I came across existentialism, an extremely diverse philosophical movement that places emphasis on individual existence, freedom and choice.

Søren Kierkegaard, a 19th century philosopher, is regarded as the father of existentialism. It was he who maintained that *"the individual is solely responsible for giving his or her own life meaning and for living that life passionately and sincerely*, in spite of many existential obstacles and distractions including despair, angst, absurdity, alienation and boredom." [219]

---

[218] *Are You Ready To Take The Cosmic Plunge?* article accessed on July 30, 2011 at http://www.kachina.net/~alunajoy/2011-jan1.html
[219] http://en.wikipedia.org/wiki/Existentialism

I totally concur with this proposal.

I am responsible for attaching meaning to my life, for locating my passions and inspirations, and for living all with genuineness, honesty and sincerity.

It appears that subsequent existentialist philosophers "retain the emphasis on the individual, but differ, in varying degrees, on how one achieves and what constitutes a fulfilling life, what obstacles must be overcome, and what external and internal factors are involved, including the potential consequences of the existence or non-existence of God." [220]

These differences make sense when embracing such a movement because, while we are all connected to each other, we have also chosen to become individuated aspects of the same, meaning that your experience(s) will always differ from my own.

---

[220] http://en.wikipedia.org/wiki/Existentialism

Existentialists believe that "most people do not live a real life, but some sort of pseudo-life that fails to get to the heart of a genuine human existence." [221]

They also believe that "most people fail to be truly themselves, by thoughtlessly accepting the precepts and patterns of their native culture, by automatically conforming to what "one" is supposed to do, by excessively busying themselves with mundane matters and trivial concerns, or by seeking shelter from the threatening emptiness and nihilism of modern life in some established cult or religion." [222]

In short, life, if it is to be deemed authentic, "cannot be lived by following the run of any kind of "herd" and its collective beliefs and preoccupations." [223]

I found it most intriguing to discover that the teachings of Buddha have been considered a forerunner of existentialism.

---

[221] *Sartre: Existentialism and The Modern World* article accessed on July 30, 2011 at
http://faculty.frostburg.edu/phil/forum/Existentialism.htm
[222] Ibid.
[223] Ibid.

A central proposition of existentialism is that "the human being, through their own consciousness, creates their own values and determines a meaning to their life." [224]

Which would you rather ... an opportunity to choose your own life or to have that life chosen for you?

Unfortunately, we have had to become integrated conformists, so it is only when we are able to "understand our own enculturation ... [that] we can begin to resist and transcend that socialization. [225]

Is this not beginning to sound like the choice that Neo (the main character in *The Matrix*) had to make between living honestly (the red pill) versus living in continued ignorance (the blue pill), wherein he demonstrates the agony that accompanies such a move?

---

[224] http://en.wikipedia.org/wiki/Existentialism
[225] *Becoming More Authentic: The Positive Side of Existentialism* article accessed on July 31, 2011 at http://www.tc.umn.edu/~parkx032/CY-AU.html

Existentialists "define authenticity as a state in which the individual is aware of the true nature of the human condition. In contrast, inauthenticity is defined as a state in which the individual is either ignorant of the true nature of reality or in denial with respect to it." [226]

Does this not sound like the beginnings of a spiritual awakening to you?

---

[226] Irwin, William (2002) *The Matrix and Philosophy: Welcome to the Desert of the Real* (page 166). Peru, IL: Open Court Publishing Company.

There is an ancient proverb that "reminds us that only brave souls walk the human path, for the earthly existence is enshrouded in a veil of illusion. Choosing to walk a spiritual path provides an opportunity to live life with an open heart. Living open heartedly means we must fearlessly face our old patterns, transform self sabotage and bring the light of conscious awareness to our shadow. This is a lifelong excursion." [227]

In the words of Pierre Teilhard de Chardin, a French Jesuit priest who was also trained as both a paleontologist as well as a philosopher ... *We are not human beings having a spiritual experience; we are spiritual beings having a human experience.*

As long as we continue to exist in the physical realm, we cannot deny our humanity; instead, we are here to embrace it, wholeheartedly, while living fully in the now.

---

[227] *The Spiritual Path of An Open Heart* article accessed on July 30, 2011 at http://www.authenticityassociates.com/the-spiritual-path-of-an-open-heart

It was Abraham Maslow, an American Psychologist, who believed we could become more self-actualized if we pursued "meanings and values beyond ourselves and our families," [228] thereby transcending our concerns for "what other people think and focus instead on being the persons we choose to be." [229]

Remaining true to yourself, remaining true to your own truth(s), while also making use of discernment, is what constitutes your authenticity. It must also be remembered that truth(s) are variable from person to person.

Should you come face to face with a truth that does not resonate with your own (and by resonating, I am referring to the deep goosebumpy feelings you immediately receive upon recognizing your truth), you simply agree to disagree, as goes one of our favorite sayings, and then move on.

---

[228] *Becoming More Authentic: The Positive Side of Existentialism* article accessed on July 31, 2011 at http://www.tc.umn.edu/~parkx032/CY-AU.html
[229] Ibid.

Everyone is on their own authentic journey, at their own juncture, within their own development and perspective. This is to be respected.

You are not here to judge.

You are not here to condemn.

Instead, you are here to make choices that will strengthen and enhance your own individual growth.

Canada has long been referenced as a cultural melting pot whereby peoples of diverse nationalities, ethnic groups and religious affiliations can come together.

Life would be incredibly dull if we all looked the same, talked the same, thought the same; hence, diversity, in this manner, serves to enrich our lives.

It becomes in both learning to recognize our similarities while also appreciating our differences, that, together, we can overcome prejudice and intolerance, working towards a more peaceful and productive world.

Unfortunately, diversity is a reality that is also feared, mainly because we can become too complacent when we become accustomed to the way things are, to the way things have always been.

Change, for the most part, puts a great many people on the defensive.

Education, then, is what "universalizes the human spirit. You cannot be universalized if you are only in one world, the world of your ethnic group, the world of your neighborhood, the world of your religion, or the world of your family. The word 'university' is related to this idea. Our lives are enhanced when we understand and appreciate many worlds. It has been said that if you gain a new language, you gain a new world. I believe that the reverse is also true: if you lose a language, you lose a world. When our spirit is universalized, we can cross boundaries and feel comfortable in other worlds. We can teach and learn from others in a mutually supportive effort to acquire a profound respect for the human condition." [230]

These words, belonging to Dr. Samuel Betances, professor emeritus at Northeastern Illinois University, noted author and lecturer, certainly give one much to reflect upon.

---

[230] *Cultural Diversity: Towards A Whole Society* article accessed on July 31, 2011 at
http://www.ccsf.edu/Resources/Tolerance/lessons/div01.html

Psychologists tells us that where we are born, how we are brought up, the values we grow up with (based on the beliefs of family) and the systems of education we are exposed to, all have an enormous influence on our thinking, which, in turn, is directed related to both how we perceive reality and what we perceive reality to be.

The first place we must begin, whilst on the spiritual path, lies in questioning the beliefs that we were raised in (which are also perceived as being a significant part of our cultural identity).

The unified field of consciousness is "the essence and source of creation of everyone, regardless of race, age, gender, background, richness or poverty; place and time. Whatever we individually think, experience or believe, we are all conscious beings sharing the same essence." [231]

---

[231] The Unified Field – The Consciousness of All Creation website accessed on March 17, 2011 at
http://www.anunda.com/paradigm/unified-field.htm

However, it becomes the beliefs that we have about ourselves, the beliefs to which we have become ingrained and attached, that create the sense of separation that is felt. Clearly, *we are the source of our own perceived limitations.*

We are privileged to live in a world that has been infused with a vital, living, conscious, infinite, fluid (malleable) energy. As vital, living, conscious and infinite beings, capable of change, we, too, are this same energy.

Life experiences are created by beliefs, imaginations, and emotions, all of which work together as one system. Emotions (energy in motion), however, are the links that exist between the body, mind and spirit; an affiliation that must now be forged anew.

It is imperative that you learn to analyze (in a detached way) and challenge your beliefs. It is as equally important that you detach yourself from the hardened belief systems that continue to generate superstition, bias, discrimination, bigotry, intolerance, chauvinism, prejudice, ignorance, irrationality and premature (and sometimes perverse) conclusions.

Learning to release yourself from these negative outcomes is what shall begin to transform your inner world.

As you work toward attaining the inner peace (emotional freedom) that is needed, you are achieving self-healing.

It is also imperative to remember that as individual consciousness grows, so, too, does this affect the collective consciousness in a positive way.

*Anything that you do to enhance your life in the here and now, can only serve to also benefit the unified field to which we are all connected.*

We are here to respect our individuated differences; we are here to embrace empathy and compassion; we are here to create connections (inclusiveness) and a sense of belonging.

It is so true when Dr. Steven Greer shares that "the entirety of creation is sacred and every being is sacred, because spirit, the awake Being, is the very fabric of all that there is. And it is always perfectly one, even if it's playing and displaying upon itself as if it is different. The challenge is to see the oneness within the difference, and also enjoy the difference." [232]

Therein lies the diversity, n'est-ce pas?

Vive la différence!

---

[232] Greer, Steven. (2006). *Hidden Truth - Forbidden Knowledge* (p 270). Crozet, VA: Crossing Point, Inc.

You are not here to focus on the suffering and the misery that exists within this illusion, thereby adding to both the negativity and gravity of the situation. Instead, you are here to take enough interest in the game of life (or divine drama, if you would rather), playing the game consciously in order to achieve the overall purpose ... enlightenment.

We are a melding of *God-man* (the mind of God expressing in human form) and *man-God* (physical man expressing the God within), a combined merger of spiritual and physical that serves to continue the expansion of the Father into forever.

It becomes in the realization, and employment, of our truest nature that God meets God. [233]

We are *continually evolving and changing* as per our own individual experience(s).

---

[233] Beckow, Steve. *The Game of Life* article accessed on July 31, 2011 at http://stevebeckow.com/2010/11/the-game-of-life/

This also adds to both the greater collective experience as well as the totality of God, which means, as well, that *God is also continually evolving and changing.*

How could it be otherwise for this loving energy that is ongoing and forever?

God loves us so grandly that we have been allowed, through choice and free will, to create our vast illusions of perfection and imperfection, good and evil, positive and negative.

This means something that many people are not yet ready for … it means that God, being the totality of All That Is, is the wrong *as well as* the right, the vile ugliness *as well as* the alluring beauty, the unholiness *as well as* the divinity, the illusion *as well as* the reality.

Truly, there is no greater love than this.

We have been entrusted with the power(s) to create that which will enable us to *expand in our knowingness.*

God allows us to express as we choose, without judgment.

We determine and select which path(s) to take, remembering that the primary tool for this journey is naught but life itself.

Aside from love on an immaculately grand scale, what else holds matter together?

The answer to this question is thought ... for this, too, is what God is.

It is known that *thought must first exist before manifestation of thought* (creation) *can take place.* In that alignment, we have the ability to manifest whatever we wish, all for the sole purpose of enhancing the wisdom that we continue to accrue, life after life after life.

We create our lives through our own thought processes. Everything you think, you will feel. Everything you feel, you will manifest. Everything you manifest serves to create the condition(s) of your life.

Every word you utter expresses some feeling within your soul. Every word you utter serves to create the conditions of your life. This is a direct fusion of thought with emotion.

Thought is the true giver of life that never dies, that can never be destroyed. All have used it to think themselves into life, for *thought is your link to the mind of God.*

We get what we speak. We are what we think. We become what we direct our energies to. We become that which we conclude ourselves to be.

We are the creators and directors of our lives. We write the script and decide who plays the roles assigned to them.

As I have shared in all of my previous works, "everything that you see, you experience, you feel in your external world, is always a reflection of what you are feeling in your inside world. You can easily experience peace and tranquility around you if you choose to focus on peace and tranquility. The single and most important thing that you can do to help Mother Earth and the people and beings of your planet is to create peace, harmony and love there." [234]

---

[234] Beckow, Steve. *The Arcturian Circle: How We Create Our Reality* article accessed on June 28, 2011 at
http://stevebeckow.com/2011/04/the-arcturian-circle/

Changing the world around you cannot be done from the outside; instead, all change must first begin, with the individual, on the inside.

As you become more mindful of your day to day experience(s), you also come to realize that you have created everything that surrounds you in this life, all through a matching vibrational attraction.

As I have stated many times before, we are vibrational beings, living in a vibrational world, a world that can also be viewed as a magnetic world (for comparative purposes) whereby those things with a similar vibration (thoughts, feelings and acts of observation) are automatically attracted to each other.

Most of you are familiar with the *like attracts like* statement. In essence, this is exactly what we are addressing here. This is what leads us to one of the most difficult pieces of the life puzzle that we must come to terms with: the fact that *we have created that which exists for us in this life* (outside of the conditions into which we have been born, of course).

The moment you realize that you are the creator of your own world is the very moment that you become aware, that you become a conscious creator.

Creating from a conscious perspective means creating with positive action (meaning purpose and intent), with passion, and with happiness.

In fact, this becomes the illuminating *aha* moment that Oprah always speaks about.

In becoming aware of your ability to create, as a conscious creator, you also take full ownership and responsibility for that which you are creating.

The more you "focus on what you love, the more you will see things to love. This is where you begin to become very aware of thinking and feeling and putting your attention on that which you love, so it can be magnified. You have an awareness that you are choosing to focus on all that you love. When you do this for yourself and for your own reality, magnetically your reality begins to change. As your reality begins to change, so do other people's realities." [235]

There is another introspective way to look at this. You need to begin to see "each person, each object, each situation around you acting as mirrors or reflective devices ... all reflecting back to you that which they see. So if a person comes into your life and they are angry, they are simply reflecting back to you something that is within you. A person cannot reflect anger back to you, if none exists within you. The same is true for love. This is also the reason that your car breaks down or you get stuck in traffic when you are already in a bad mood. *You cannot attract anything into your reality that does not already exist inside of you.* That is why we suggest that you become very aware of what you see in your reality and become very selective in what you choose to magnify. When you see and feel what you love, we want you to be so aware of that so you can magnify it exponentially. You see, *your emotions are the fuel that*

---

[235] Beckow, Steve. *The Arcturian Circle: How We Create Our Reality* article accessed on June 28, 2011 at http://stevebeckow.com/2011/04/the-arcturian-circle/

*magnifies your creations.* Be grateful and appreciate when you see what you love in your reality. Your gratitude and appreciation will magnify it and attract more of it into your experience." [236]

Anything that serves to create life-enhancing feelings (responses), such as peace, joy, compassion, appreciation and gratitude, will also have a strong, positive, effect on the physical body.

On the flip side, anything that serves to create life-restricting feelings (responses), such as tension, anger, fear, frustration, anxiety and depression, will have the opposite effect.

You (and only you) are more than capable of making a conscious decision as to what specific feelings *you* wish to experience. Merely reacting to subconscious fears and anxieties, only serves to keep you enslaved to a power that exists outside of yourself.

---

[236] Beckow, Steve. *The Arcturian Circle: How We Create Our Reality* article accessed on June 28, 2011 at
http://stevebeckow.com/2011/04/the-arcturian-circle/

It is indeed possible to change your perception, to change your awareness, to change your experience, but it requires both diligence and positive action. In essence, this process of needed change is an internal one.

When you become attuned to source energy, the energy of the unified field of which we are a significant part, the intelligent energy that we also refer to as God, then you are truly living the life you are meant to live.

From a deeply metaphysical point of view, upon reaching and maintaining a mindful state on a daily basis (completely achieving the state of a detached observer), you become, in essence, the unified field (God) becoming aware of itself, do you not?

As Kevin Schoeninger so aptly puts it ... "to experience this insight, imagine that when you are breathing, the Universe is breathing you. When you are taking action, you are The Field acting through you." [237]

---

[237] Schoeninger, Kevin. (2007) *The Power of Practice: A Practical Guide to Health, Happiness, and The Life You Are Meant To Live* (page 54).

In essence, then, you are God experiencing life on the physical plane. Every personal thought, every personal feeling, every personal act of observation, therefore, also involves God acting through you.

The power operating within you is the same power that operates within this remarkably vast and majestic universe.

Despite your shared connection to the unified field, to the All That Is, you also maintain your own unique perspective, in that no one thinks the exact same thoughts in the exact same manner as yourself; likewise, no one expresses the exact same feelings in the exact same manner.

I see this as equating to the fact that that each of us are individuated aspects of God, existing here, now, so that we may experience ourselves fully, and in all ways.

While I may have dreamed of being a rock star in my earlier years, personal experiences (all of which include genetics, personality, upbringing, conscious desires and intentions, subconscious aversions and fears, interest as well as intuition) were to dictate otherwise.

Clearly, there are some things that I am better able and qualified to do than others, so this is where I need to place my focus.

With a flair for the written word, writing has become such an important and integral part of my life, that I would feel lost if I did not continue to express myself in this way. It has become through my research writing that I have discovered my gift, my passion, my joy, my bliss.

You, too, have a specific gift to offer the world.

It is up to you to discover that which you have the aptitude, love and interest for. This, then, becomes an internal focus, for therein lies your gift, your contribution, the thrill and joy of the experience.

When you are *in the zone* or *in the groove*, as it has also been described, you are *in the enjoyable and fun-filled now*.

Remembering that we are all a part of the same unified field, anything that serves to benefit one, through such an engagement process, always serves to benefit the many as well. This is what you are here to remember.

You are also here to figure out what fills you with inherent joy and makes you feel good, thereby committing yourself to its manifestation.

This might mean exercising on a regular basis, meditating on a daily basis, preparing nutritious meals, taking the time to de-stress, spending more time in nature and making sure that you are getting adequate rest. After securing your immediate personal needs, you are able to expand outward to lovingly encompass both family and work.

Thereafter, you attempt to do what you can also do for the betterment of the macrocosm (the bigger picture), courtesy of your talents and gifts.

It is essential that you take the time to become involved in something that you love to do, whatever that may be, *on a daily basis*, for therein you will find both inspiration and a renewed sense of enthusiasm and rejuvenation. These are the feelings that I experience when writing (reading and researching are also focal aspects as well) on a daily basis. Likewise, when I take the time to complete a 45 minute workout on my treadmill, I feel euphoric.

When you are doing something that feels right, know that you have made the best choice for you.

If you feel relaxed and yet focused (aware), passionate and yet energized, while also feeling balanced (all courtesy of the sense of inner direction that prevails), you can rest assured that your intuition has directed you thusly.

Likewise, when there exists synergy and flow, meaning that everything just fits perfectly well together and the right circumstances are finding their way to you, know that you are on the correct path for yourself.

There exists a divine purpose for everything and you, my friend, have an integral part to play in discovering just what that purpose may be for you, at any given time.

When you are able to reap the benefits from your actions, know that this, too, is a tangible result.

If ever you make a choice that produces immediate inner tension, frustration and anxiety, know that you have made the wrong choice for you.

If ever you make a choice based upon what you feel (believe) someone else wants you to make, know that you are making the wrong choice for you.

If ever you make a choice based on insecurity and fear (which can also mean the need to defend yourself), know that you have made the wrong choice for you.

If ever you make a choice that leads you further and further away from that which makes you feel whole and complete, know that you have made the wrong choice for you.

On an energetic level of being, you are able to intuit the best intentions, thoughts, feelings and actions for yourself in the here and now.

When you believe, in both body and mind, what the heart (soul) feels, thereby acting on this belief, fully incorporating all three integral and interconnected aspects on a daily basis, investing in your innate divine being while feeling peace, acceptance, appreciation and gratitude, all can be made real.

As stated before, in knowing that we are all a part of the same unified field, anything that serves to benefit one also serves to benefit the all.

Choosing what one loves to do, in all aspects of their life, makes for a much happier, more relaxed, more contented, individual.

When deciding on a career based solely on what you love to do, know that the money will follow because of the energetic vibratory nature of the joy and awareness involved (which also equates to choosing based on internal need as opposed to external need).

You simply have to trust in the process, as it is a total belief in yourself, a belief without doubt, that serves to create the richest, and most fertile, soil upon which to sow your deepest desires.

Creating your ideal life, a little bit every day, is the way in which to begin.

[1] Learn to become more aware of your choices so that you become a deliberate and conscious creator as opposed to creating by unconscious default.

[2] Learn to replace all negative and fearful intentions, thoughts, words and actions with positive ones, through whichever means present themselves to you.

[3] Take the time to understand who you are and why you are here, accepting that you have an important purpose for this life (as does everyone else).

[4] Learn to detach from emotional triggers and attachments (such as guilt and fear) in order to cultivate compassion on a deep and everlasting level.

[5] Learn to become more mindful of living in the now, seizing the moment each and every day, knowing that every positive action not only improves your life, but that it also serves to improve things for the greater collective whole (the unified field).

[6] Accept and take responsibility for your actions, knowing that you alone are responsible for everything that you create.

[7] Make a conscious effort to ensure that your intentions, thoughts, feelings, and actions are always in alignment (vibrational agreement) in order to better support what you choose to create

[8] Learn to trust both the universe, as well as your intuitive self, knowing that living from a heart-based consciousness will always serve your higher aspirations.

In the words of Andrew Cohen (editor of EnlightenNext Magazine) … *Spiritual maturity is not a matter of how long you have lived or even how much life experience you have. The important question is: how much does any of us actually* learn *from our life experience? Those people who are more spiritually developed are people who have been deeply paying attention, who are sensitive and awake enough to truly learn, and grow, and significantly evolve as a result of the life experience that they have.*

It was on Coast to Coast AM that scientist David Sereda provided evidence that "our Solar System entered a new field of cosmic energy that set off a chain of events [all of which include] ... [1] the vibration of the entire planet, [2] the largest storm ever recorded on Saturn, and [3] an early sunrise in Greenland (related to a wobble of the Earth and magnetic pole movement)," [238] a sequence of events that were noted on December 22, 2010, courtesy of earthquake sensors.

It was Einstein who said that "the field is the sole governing agency of matter. Fields of energy dictate the behavior of everything – from subatomic particles to massive planets.

---

[238] Conscious Life News (February 5, 2011). *Scientific Proof that Galactic Energies Have Triggered Worldwide Consciousness Expansion* article accessed on June 27, 2011 at http://consciouslifenews.com/scientific-proof-galactic-energies-triggered-worldwide-consciousness-expansion/114819/

When you see a sudden change in an energy system, it will cause a sudden change to an ecosystem." [239]

Knowing that the human body has an electromagnetic field that "can be affected by activity on the sun, as well as energies coming from the galactic center, as the Earth moves through it," [240] it was also Sereda who pointed out "that if these energy fields that are coming in from the galactic center contain harmonic information, then there is absolutely *no doubt that you can scientifically prove* that it is causing a consciousness shift on this planet and will continue to do so through 2012." [241]

Of the many proposed theories for 2012, it is the Mayan elders who share that we are going to receive new energy that will cause a shift in consciousness, affecting everything on the planet, including Mother Earth herself.

---

[239] Conscious Life News (February 5, 2011). *Scientific Proof that Galactic Energies Have Triggered Worldwide Consciousness Expansion* article accessed on June 27, 2011 at http://consciouslifenews.com/scientific-proof-galactic-energies-triggered-worldwide-consciousness-expansion/114819/
[240] Ibid.
[241] Ibid.

Bruce Lipton, an internationally recognized leader in bridging science and spirit, has said that "consciousness tells energy to tell the DNA what to do." [242] By this he means that your genes are not your blueprint; rather, it is consciousness that is your blueprint. Therefore, it is likely that, "along with a shift in consciousness, our DNA will be upgraded" [243] as well.

Confirmed by both science as well as the events that are currently unfolding around the world, it has become clear that a worldwide consciousness expansion is happening now and will continue through to 2012.

Ascension is "an incremental process that happens in stages." [244]

---

[242] Conscious Life News (February 5, 2011). *Scientific Proof that Galactic Energies Have Triggered Worldwide Consciousness Expansion* article accessed on June 27, 2011 at http://consciouslifenews.com/scientific-proof-galactic-energies-triggered-worldwide-consciousness-expansion/114819/
[243] Ibid.
[244] Wilcock, David. *Disclosure War at Critical Mass: Birds, Fish and Political Death, Part 1* article accessed on June 27, 2011 at http://stevebeckow.com/2011/01/david-wilcock-disclosure-war-critical-mass-birds-fish-political-deaths-part-1/

As such, ascension is also completely unique to each individual in that "the discovery of divinity and the movement toward that energy is a completely individualized experience." [245]

The experience is a moving one, a pertinent one, a surrendering one, a deeply profound and transformative one; an inspiring experiencing pertaining to each individual in question. [246] The experience is also a natural one, part of one's inevitable journey back to the nature of our very selves, our divine selves; an "endless journey from God back to God again." [247]

---

[245] Wilcock, David. *Disclosure War at Critical Mass: Birds, Fish and Political Death, Part 1* article accessed on June 27, 2011 at http://stevebeckow.com/2011/01/david-wilcock-disclosure-war-critical-mass-birds-fish-political-deaths-part-1/

[246] Wilcock, David. *Disclosure War at Critical Mass: Birds, Fish and Political Death, Part 3* article accessed on June 27, 2011 at http://stevebeckow.com/2011/01/david-wilcock-disclosure-war-critical-mass-birds-fish-political-deaths-part-33/

[247] Beckow, Steve. *On Ascension (Part 5): What is the Nature of the Light Uplifting Earth?* article accessed on June 27, 2011 at http://stevebeckow.com/2011/02/ascension-part-5-nature-light-uplifting-earth/

Ascension is an ongoing process. Ascension is *not* an upward movement; likewise, ascension is *not* a spiritual judgment process. [248] In short, ascension is able to take place due to our raised vibrations.

As further shared by Steve Beckow, "in the course of our descent into duality, we forgot everything about our earlier existence and identified with the lower vibrations" [249] knowing that this "third dimension of reality was created for us to experience." [250]

While we were never meant to remain here for an indefinite period of time, we elected to incarnate here in order to experience the full totality of our very selves.

In truth, we have been living in a reality that we, ourselves, have created; a reality of both duality and polarity.

---

[248] Beckow, Steve. *On Ascension (Part 3): What is the Golden Age?* article accessed on June 27, 2011 at
http://stevebeckow.com/2011/02/ascension-part-3-golden-age/
[249] Beckow, Steve. *On Ascension (Part 1): Where Did We Descend From?* article accessed on June 27, 2011 at
http://stevebeckow.com/2011/02/ascension-part-1-descend/
[250] Ibid.

Duality refers to physical separateness of opposite, yet related, modes of being: male and female, light and dark, night and day, yin and yang, hot and cold, past and future.

Polarity, on the other hand, refers to the essence of the underlying unity of these dualistic pairs, meaning that you cannot have one creative force without the other; that both are needed to maintain creative balance; that both are merely two extremes of the same thing.

As a result, we were gifted with the opportunity to view ourselves from a different perspective, all of which was deemed both necessary and important if we were to truly know, understand and master ourselves in all ways.

Likewise, we were offered the opportunity to *transcend polarity while still living within the polarity*, a decision that enables you to move forward with a life filled with freedom, resolution and peace.

Clearly, each has served to contribute to the expansion of planetary consciousness.

As you expand in your awareness, you come to realize that "what you believe, how you feel, and the attitudes you espouse directly affect the personal energy field which surrounds you, and this in turn impinges on and affects the energy fields of those with whom you interact. Consequently, if you change any of your beliefs, feelings, or attitudes it alters the effect you have on others and how they respond to you." [251]

*The awakening has reached people who have no direct interest or knowledge of Ascension, yet their senses tell them what has been wrong for a long time, and if Man is to go forward changes must take place. Suddenly the group consciousness is expanding and moving into the Light, which is inspiring people to achieve greater things for the good of all.* [252]

---

[251] Smallman, John. *Saul: Changing Your Beliefs Alters Your Effect On Others* article accessed on June 27, 2011 at http://stevebeckow.com/2011/02/saul-changing-beliefs-alters-effect/
[252] Beckow, Steve. *On Ascension (Part 5): What is the Nature of the Light Uplifting Earth?* article accessed on June 27, 2011 at http://stevebeckow.com/2011/02/ascension-part-5-nature-light-uplifting-earth/

As Steve Beckow also shares ... "enlightenment is the purpose of life. Enlightenment is the realization of our true identity as God (or I could have said as Light) which comes about as the result of our being given and assimilating light in the [course of the] experience."[253]

Love is the very energy that is bringing about the pertinent, and much needed, changes. Might love, then, be defined as the very galactic wave (the Intelligent Design of which, we, too, are a glorious part) that is commandeering us to the next level: one of peace, freedom, compassion, fraternity, purity, intelligence, creativity, liberation, transformation, harmony, love, acceptance, unlimited beauty, virtue, new life, respect, tolerance, sharing, gratitude and forgiveness?

It is essential that you "do not buy into the doom, gloom, danger, and protection racket which is used to encourage and maintain fear and mistrust, because it affects your energy fields very negatively, causing others to feel

---

[253] Beckow, Steve. *On Ascension (Part 5): What is the Nature of the Light Uplifting Earth?* article accessed on June 27, 2011 at http://stevebeckow.com/2011/02/ascension-part-5-nature-light-uplifting-earth/

threatened by you. Instead, focus intently on your desire to be as God created you: loving peaceful presences, and intend to share and extend that energy at all times [so that you can] then enjoy the positive results it brings into your lives." [254]

There will, however, still be negative and unpleasant experiences due to the fact that "many people live in fear and on the defensive, ready to attack at a moment's notice. Be compassionate and ask for spiritual guidance (always readily available) when these kinds of situations arise, and then respond appropriately instead of being drawn back into these painful games that the illusion supports and encourages [in order] to maintain itself." [255]

It has always been the intent of humanity to "move out of the Illusion and into Reality, and each one of you has your

---

[254] Smallman, John. *Saul: Changing Your Beliefs Alters Your Effect On Others* article accessed on June 27, 2011 at http://stevebeckow.com/2011/02/saul-changing-beliefs-alters-effect/

[255] Ibid.

own essential, individual part to play in this momentous event, because by playing your part you make it happen." [256]

Doing what you love will allow you to remain within the much needed higher state of joy.

It is also imperative that you remain calm, for in so doing you are not adding to the emotional turmoil that is being created, all courtesy of the doom, gloom, danger and protection racket of which John Smallman speaks.

It also becomes in rejecting both the rumors as well as the disinformation that you are able to remain calm.

In visualizing the positive outcome, you must stand firm in your resolve. It is my belief that a happy life will grow out of the current chaos.

As Steve Beckow writes, it is up to us "to protect the Earth's wellbeing, during this time of trouble, by remaining as far as

---

[256] Smallman, John. *Saul: Changing Your Beliefs Alters Your Effect On Others* article accessed on June 27, 2011 at http://stevebeckow.com/2011/02/saul-changing-beliefs-alters-effect/

possible strong, immovable, and calm," [257] as this will help to keep our vibrations high.

You really can succeed in changing yourself from being fearful to being loving. It will be in having done so that you are able to "demonstrate to all with whom you interact that it can be done, and it reduces your levels of stress and brings you peace. They see this in the happy, competent, and sane way that you live and operate; and you will experience a pleased acceptance of yourself by others because of this. You are, each one of you, consciously intending and being loving and peaceful presences, thus changing the world and dissolving the illusion. For this you are greatly honored." [258]

The entire game is changing. Clearly, it is time for us to be *getting out of our own way.*

---

[257] Beckow, Steve. *Keep Calm and Don't Add to the Emotional Turmoil Being Generated* article accessed on June 27, 2011 at http://stevebeckow.com/2011/02/calm-add-emotional-turmoil-generated/
[258] Smallman, John. *Saul: Changing Your Beliefs Alters Your Effect On Others* article accessed on June 27, 2011 at http://stevebeckow.com/2011/02/saul-changing-beliefs-alters-effect/

As you make the changes within, so, too, is your personal paradigm changing. In reference to the continuing changes in consciousness, we are already on our way to developing a more harmonious relationship with each other. While it is true that "staying calm in all situations is not going to be easy," [259] each can do their best, in this way, to bring about the peace on Earth that has been foretold, the peace that we have longed dreamed and visualized for ourselves.

You, too, are here to become a "passionate explorer of the mysteries of existence" [260] so that you may also report back from your "expeditions into the uncharted regions of consciousness," [261] thereby offering a potential roadmap to fellow explorers.

In a race to the finish line, a race that all shall win, a race that we have already won, the question becomes: are you ready to begin a new game at a higher vibration?

---

[259] Beckow, Steve. *SaLuSa: Matters Have Almost Reached Their Conclusion* article accessed on July 1, 2011 at http://stevebeckow.com/2011/07/salusa-1-july-2011/
[260] Freke, Tim. (2009) *How Long Is Now: A Journey to Enlightenment and Beyond* (page 4). Carlsbad, CA: Hay House, Inc.
[261] Ibid.

# Sing a Song

The 1970's musical group Earth, Wind & Fire [262] have always been a favorite of mine, with key, upbeat, and meaningful lyrics, as written for *Sing a Song* (refer to their 1975 album entitled Gratitude); lyrics which are clearly still relevant to today.

*When you feel down and out; Sing a song, it'll make your day. Here's a time to shout; Sing a song, it'll make a way. Sometimes it's hard to care; Sing a song, it'll make your day. A smile so hard to bear; Sing a song, it'll make a way.*

*Bring your heart to believing; Sing a song, it'll make your day. Life ain't about no retrieving; Sing a song, it'll make a way. Give yourself what you need; Sing a song, it'll make your day. Smile, smile, smile and believe; Sing a song, it'll make a way.*

---

[262] http://www.earthwindandfire.com/index.html

Music continues to be a means in which to uplift one's self (a form of brainwave entrainment, if you will) to a higher energy level. For example, it has been noted that music can assist with athletic achievement, with music serving to motivate the athlete (through inducing feelings of emotion that an athlete can use to their advantage).

In keeping with the beat of the music, it has been shown that slow music can slow the heartbeat, slow the breathing rate, and reduce one's blood pressure. This, of course, means that fast music serves to accomplish the opposite. When you find yourself in a lethargic slump, take the time to listen to the type of music that makes you want to dance, that makes you want to sing, and you will quickly find yourself in a much better mind space.

In truth, music is one of the few activities that involves using the whole brain; however, not all of the effects of music on the brain are positive. It has been scientifically proven that certain types of music (mainly heavy rock and rap) actually cause the brain to lose the symmetry that exists between both hemispheres.

In truth, young or old, music is an effective means of managing (and/or reducing) stress. Can it not be said, then, that music can be utilized, as an effective medium, to also facilitate a healthy existence?

As Burton Cummings shares in *My Own Way To Rock*, and it is so very true ... *I got my own way to rock, I got my own way to roll, and when you're walkin' that walk, it's good for your soul.*

# *Addendum*

As a dear friend of mine has shared ... *Unknowingly, we have all been programmed from a tender age (and sometimes even earlier). Continued through mass media, this programming greatly impacts how we live our lives. Understanding our "programs" becomes the first step towards true freedom and enlightenment.*

Each of us has been subjected to behavioral conditioning as generated mostly by parental programming.

Please understand that I am not talking about Hostile Aggressive Parenting (HAP), which leads to Parental Alienation Syndrome (PAS).

Were you, however, aware that mental health is often directly associated with parental programming?

Likewise, environmental conditions are also affiliated with parental programming, highlighting the nature versus nurture argument that always seems to continue on into infinity.

If we are to succeed in becoming who we want to be, it is imperative that we find a way to get beyond these programs of ours.

It is my belief that we are Spiritual Beings having a human experience. If we are to heal our wounded selves, much inner child work is necessary.

This is where you must become, first and foremost, an inner child detective; meaning that you need to pinpoint why you react in specific ways (to certain situations) and why you display specific feelings (such as helplessness, hopelessness, loneliness, anxiety, depression, desperation and anger) in certain situations.

It also becomes imperative to acknowledge that all core relationships with self are formed based upon a combination of role modeling (witnessed) and messages (received), all obtained, courtesy of the adults in our world.

All future relationships, then, are built upon this early childhood foundation.

The *moment you have become aware* that there is *a part of you* that *needs to be healed* is critical to the healing equation because this *also becomes a moment of acknowledgment,* fully realized or not, that *you have the power to change your relationship with self.*

An amazing process, really, the more we become aware of our own reactions, feelings and responses, from a detached point of view, so, too, are we able to stop taking the behavior of others (their reactions, feelings and responses) so personally.

As you become more aware, as you become more mindful, as you become more conscious of a new way of looking at life (which includes yourself and others), you are able to move forward.

Inner child healing is "the only way to empower ourselves to stop living life in reaction to the past. If we are going to have a chance to reverse the self destructive patterns of human kind, it is going to come from individuals healing self. By healing our inner child wounds, we can change the world." [263]

It is through healing the wounds of the inner child that you learn to love, accept and respect yourself.

As we heal ourselves, so, too, are we healing the planet.

In order to heal, *you must learn to take ownership and responsibility for your life.*

In order to heal, *you must practice the art of discernment* by identifying those things that you cannot change versus those that are within your power to do so. This can be achieved in the developing of a loving and compassionate relationship with self.

Learning to make choices from a place of love, acceptance, understanding, forgiveness and respect becomes the way to achieving inner peace.

---

[263] *Inner Child Healing* article accessed on September 9, 2011 at http://www.joy2meu.com/inner_child.html

In order to heal, *you must change the way you think.*

In order to heal, *you must change the way you respond* to situations, to people, to emotions.

In order to heal, *you must learn to detach from the wounded self* in an effort to become an objective observer (witness).

For anyone who wishes to change their behavior patterns, detachment (a process that allows you to become observer as you are thinking the thoughts and feeling the emotions) is key.

In order to heal, *you must learn to release feelings* (such as helplessness, hopelessness, loneliness, anxiety, depression, desperation and anger), otherwise they manifest outwardly as physical disease.

You must not be afraid of your feelings and emotions, for they are a part of who you are. Instead you must accept them. As you learn to feel them, without reaction (which is where the detached observer comes into play), and are present with them, they begin to dissipate. Detachment allows you to feel and then release.

Simply observing the feelings does not heal them.

First and foremost, you must acknowledge them, for they are a part of who you are. Secondly, you must begin to understand why you feel and react as you do. Lastly, while you still need to feel and experience, so, too, do you need to learn to release the emotional energy so that you may heal.

It is essential that you do not give your power away, allowing the way you are thinking and feeling to control you. However, it is equally as important that deep wounds be brought to the surface so that healing may occur. One learns, thereafter, the importance of releasing emotional related stress on a continuing basis.

Pretend that you are outside, observing the clouds as they float across the sky. Now imagine your thought forms (and feelings) as the very clouds that are passing you by. It is in coming to this realization that you can honestly say *I have become a witness to my own mind.* There may also be pictures and images that begin to filter through. Try to become a witness to these visualizations as well.

Do not engage with either the thoughts or the images. Simply accept them while remaining unattached. Do not judge them. Remember, you are merely the observer.

You may also notice your body responding (emotional reactions) to specific thought forms that are filtering through. Once again, you must step out of the emotion.

You should not allow an emotion to control you while in the physical body. You are merely the observer. You may continue to be the witness, but only without judgment.

Even though *becoming a witness* to thought forms, pictures, images and emotions, is not an easy task, it is something that *needs to be practiced every day*.

[1] For those who are successful when it comes to visualization, feel free to learn to visualize an image during introspective meditation, attaching a specific emotion to the image (be it a person or a situation). Encase this emotion inside a bubble and then let it go, watching as it travels further and further away on the wings of the wind.

[2] Writing (journaling) is a therapeutic tool used by many psychologists; a tool that can be used to ferret out hidden emotions. If there is a person associated with a specific emotion, for example, you can take the time to write that person a letter (to be destroyed sometime thereafter).

[3] Engaging in a variety of art related activities is yet another therapeutic medium that can be used: write a song, write a poem, paint (draw) a picture.

[4] Engaging in strenuous activity (such as running), that increases the blood pressure, is a good way to release pent-up emotions.

[5] Yoga teaches you how to train your body to relax.

[6] Confiding in someone, thereby articulating your experiences, can also help to you to let things go. It becomes in doing so that you are able to experience a deep sense of inner peace.

*We are not separate from the world process. In our own small way, we're all contributing to where we're going. The choices we make, the actions we take, what we say, what we don't say, are all adding to the momentum of the vast cosmic unfolding. When we really embrace the truth that we are not separate from the process that created us, then we need to become very clear about all the ways in which we are actually affecting the process, so that we can begin to more consciously impact its momentum in positive and evolutionary ways.*

Andrew Cohen (EnlightenNext Magazine)

As Earth, Wind & Fire share in *Shining Star ... You're a shining star, no matter who you are; Shining bright to see, what you can truly be.*

In the words of Ramana ... *The ordinary man lives in the brain unaware of himself in the Heart. The enlightened one lives in the Heart. When he moves about and deals with people and things, he knows that what he sees is not separate from the one Supreme Reality which he realized in the Heart as his own Self.*

As Johnny Nash wrote and performed ... *I can see clearly now, the rain has gone. I can see all obstacles in my way. Gone are the dark clouds that had me blind. It's gonna be a bright, bright sun-shiny day.*

In truth, it really *is* a bright sun-shiny day, if you so choose.

# Bibliography

Behrend, Genevieve. (1921) *Your Invisible Power* [264]

Behrend, Genevieve. (1929) *Attaining Your Desires* [265]

Bendriss, Lilli and Løken, Camillo. (2011) *The Shift in Consciousness.*

Bieber, Nancy L. (2010) *Decision Making and Spiritual Discernment: The Sacred Art of Finding Your Way.*

Caplan, Mariana. (2009) *Eyes Wide Open: Cultivating Discernment on the Spiritual Path.*

Chopra, Deepak. (2005) *Peace Is The Way: Bringing War and Violence to An End.*

Clark, Robert A. *The Christ Mind.* [266]

---

[264] http://www.successmanual.com/success-manual-your-invisible-power-by-genevieve-behrend-1921-free-ebook-download/

[265] http://www.successmanual.com/key-success-manual-attaining-desires-genevieve-behrend-free-ebook-download/

Coelho, Paulo. (1998) *The Alchemist.*

Coelho, Paulo. (2003) *Warrior Of The Light.*

Doucette, Michele. (2010) *A Travel in Time to Grand Pré.* (second edition)

Doucette, Michele. (2010) *The Ultimate Enlightenment For 2012: All We Need Is Ourselves.*

Doucette, Michele. (2010) *Turn Off The TV: Turn On Your Mind.*

Doucette, Michele. (2010) *Veracity At Its Best.*

Doucette, Michele. (2011) *Sleepers Awaken: The Time Is Now To Consciously Create Your Own Reality.*

Doucette, Michele. (2011) *Healing the Planet and Ourselves: How To Raise Your Vibration.*

Doucette, Michele. (2011) *You Are Everything: Everything Is You.*

---

[266] http://www.thechristmind.org/thechristmind.pdf

Doucette, Michele. (2011) *The Awakening of Humanity: A Foremost Necessity.*

Ford, Debbie. (2010) *The 21-Day Consciousness Cleanse: A Breakthrough Program for Connecting with Your Soul's Deepest Purpose.*

Freke, Timothy. (2005) *Lucid Living.*

Freke, Timothy. (2009) *How Long Is Now? A Journey to Enlightenment and Beyond.*

Gawain, Shakti. (1993) *Living In The Light: A Guide to Personal and Planetary Transformation.*

Gawain, Shakti. (1999) *The Four Levels of Healing.*

Gawain, Shakti. (2000) *The Path of Transformation: How Healing Ourselves Can Change The World.*

Gawain, Shakti. (2003) *Reflections in The Light: Daily Thoughts and Affirmations.*

Germer, Christopher K. (2009) *The Mindful Path to Self-Compassion: Freeing Yourself from Destructive Thoughts and Emotions.*

Gilbert, Paul. (2010) *The Compassionate Mind: A New Approach to Life's Challenges.*

Hawkins, David R. (1995) *Power vs. Force: The Hidden Determinants of Human Behavior.*

Hicks, Esther and Hicks, Jerry. (2004) *Ask and It Is Given: Learning to Manifest Your Desires.*

Hicks, Esther and Hicks, Jerry. (2004) *The Teachings of Abraham: Well-Being Cards.*

Hicks, Esther and Hicks, Jerry. (2005) *The Amazing Power of Deliberate Intent: Living the Art of Allowing.*

Hicks, Esther and Hicks, Jerry. (2006) *The Law of Attraction: The Basics of the Teachings of Abraham.*

Hicks, Esther and Hicks, Jerry. (2008) *The Astonishing Power of Emotions: Let Your Feelings Be Your Guide.*

Hicks, Esther and Hicks, Jerry. (2009) *The Vortex: Where The Law of Attraction Assembles all Cooperative Relationships.*

Koven, Jean-Claude. (2004) *Going Deeper: How To Make Sense of Your Life When Your Life Makes No Sense.*

Kribbe, Pamela. (2008) *The Jeshua Channelings: Christ Consciousness in a New Era.*

Liebert, Elizabeth. (2008) *The Way of Discernment: Spiritual Practices for Decision Making.*

Luckman, Sol. (2009) *Conscious Healing: Book One on the Renenetics Method* (second edition).

McTaggart, Lynne. (2003) *The Field: The Quest For The Secret Force Of The Universe.*

McTaggart, Lynne. (2008) *The Intention Experiment: Using Your Thoughts to Change Your Life and the World.*

McTaggart, Lynne. (2011) *The Bond: Connecting Through the Space Between Us.*

Millman, Dan. (2000) *Way of the Peaceful Warrior*.

Millman, Dan. (1991) *Sacred Journey of the Peaceful Warrior*.

Millman, Dan. (1992) *No ordinary Moments: A Peaceful Warrior's Guide to Daily Life*.

Millman, Dan. (1995) *The Life You Were Born To Live*.

Millman, Dan. (1999) *Everyday Enlightenment*.

Neff, Kristin. (2011) *Self-Compassion: Stop Beating Yourself Up and Leave Insecurity Behind*,

Orloff, Judith. (2009) *Emotional Repair Kit: 50 Tools To Liberate Yourself From Negative Emotions*.

Orloff, Judith. (2005) *Positive Energy: 10 Extraordinary Prescriptions for Transforming Fatigue, Stress and Fear into Vibrance, Strength and Love*.

Osho. (2007) *Emotional Wellness: Transforming Fear, Anger and Jealousy Into Creative Energy*.

Peirce, Penney. (2009) *Frequency: The Power of Personal Vibration.*

Rennison, Susan Joy. (2008) *Tuning the Diamonds: Electromagnetism and Spiritual Evolution.*

Ruiz, Don Miguel. (1997) *The Four Agreements: A Practical Guide to Personal Freedom.*

Ruiz, Don Miguel. (1999) *The Mastery of Love: A Practical Guide to The Art of Relationship.*

Ruiz, Don Miguel. (2000) *The Four Agreements Companion Book.*

Ruiz, Don Miguel. (2004) *The Voice of Knowledge: A Practical Guide to Inner Peace.*

Ruiz, Don Miguel. (2009) *Fifth Agreement: A Practical Guide to Self-Mastery.*

Sasson, Remez. *Peace of Mind in Daily Life* [267]

Stibal, Vianna. (2011) *Theta Healing: Introducing an Extraordinary Energy Healing Modality.*

Targ, Russell and Katra, Jane. (1999) *Miracles of Mind: Exploring Nonlocal Consciousness and Spiritual Healing.*

Tolle, Eckhart. (2008) *A New Earth: Awakening to Your Life's Purpose.*

Troward, Thomas. (1917) *The Law and the Word* [268]

Wilcock, David. *The Shift of the Ages – Convergence Volume One* (online book) [269]

Wilcock, David. *The Science of Oneness – Convergence Volume Two* (online book) [270]

---

[267] http://www.successconsciousness.com/books/peace-of-mind-in-daily-life.htm

[268] http://www.successmanual.com/free-success-ebook-law-and-the-word-thomas-troward/

[269] http://divinecosmos.com/start-here/books-free-online/18-the-shift-of-the-ages

Wilcock, David. *The Divine Cosmos – Convergence Volume Three* (online book) [271]

Wilcock, David. *Wanderer Awakening: The Life Story of David Wilcock* (online book) [272]

Wilcock, David. *The Reincarnation of Edgar Cayce* (online book) [273]

Wilcock, David. *The End of Our Century* (online book edited by David Wilcock) [274]

Wilcock, David. (2011) *The Source Field Investigations: The Hidden Science and Lost Civilizations Behind the 2012 Prophecies.*

---

[270] http://divinecosmos.com/start-here/books-free-online/19-the-science-of-oneness

[271] http://divinecosmos.com/start-here/books-free-online/20-the-divine-cosmos

[272] http://divinecosmos.com/start-here/books-free-online/25-wander-awakening-the-life-story-of-david-wilcock

[273] http://divinecosmos.com/start-here/books-free-online/22-the-reincarnation-of-edgar-cayce-draft-of-pt-1

[274] http://divinecosmos.com/start-here/books-free-online/26-the-end-of-our-century

## 2012

2012: The Return to Camelot [275]

The 2012 Enigma (free full length documentary) [276]

The Psychics of 2012 [277]

## Ascension

Fear Processing Exercise [278]

The Ascension Papers [279]

The Ascension Process [280]

---

[275] http://www.divinecosmos.com/videos/free-videos-online/503-amazing-free-2-hour-video-2012-return-to-camelot

[276] http://www.divinecosmos.com/index.php?option=com_content&task=view&id=374&Itemid=70

[277] http://montalk.net/science/136/the-physics-of-2012

[278] http://ascension101.com/en/ascension-tools/33-ascension-tools/105-fear-processing-exercise.html

[279] http://www.zingdad.com/blog/116-the-ascension-papers.html

[280] http://www.bibliotecapleyades.net/ascension/esp_ascension_12.htm

The Divine Dispensations (Part 1) [281]

The Divine Dispensations (Part 2) [282]

The Divine Dispensations (Part 3) [283]

The Divine Dispensations (Part 4) [284]

**Channeled Material** (worth investigating)

John Smallman [285]

Lee Carroll: Kryon Channelings [286]

Lee Carroll: The Lightworker's Handbook [287]

---

[281] http://goldenagejourney.blogspot.com/2010/10/divine-dispensations-part-1.html
[282] http://goldenagejourney.blogspot.com/2010/10/divine-dispensations-part-2.html
[283] http://goldenagejourney.blogspot.com/2010/10/divine-dispensations-part-3.html
[284] http://goldenagejourney.blogspot.com/2010/10/divine-dispensations-part-4.html
[285] http://johnsmallman.wordpress.com/
[286] http://www.kryon.com/k_25.html
[287] http://www.kryon.com/k_25b.html

Matthew Ward [288]

Mike Quinsey [289]

Pamela Kribbe: The Jeshua Channelings [290]

The Crossroads of Planetary Destiny [291]

## Consciousness Raising

A Golden Age May Be Just Around The Corner [292]

Alliance for A New Humanity [293]

Alliance for Lucid Living (Timothy Freke) [294]

---

[288] http://www.matthewbooks.com/mattsmessage.htm

[289]
http://www.treeofthegoldenlight.com/First_Contact/Channeled_Messages_by_Mike_Quinsey.htm

[290] http://www.jeshua.net/

[291] http://montalk.net/metaphys/77/the-crossroads-of-planetary-destiny

[292] http://www.huffingtonpost.com/david-wilcock/ufos-government_b_933641.html#s336273&title=What_is_consciousness

[293] http://www.anhglobal.org/

[294] http://www.theall.org/

Association for Global New Thought [295]

Awakening ezine (Ben Arion) [296]

Awakening Into Awareness ezine [297]

Be The Change [298]

Campaign for Forgiveness Research [299]

Center for Non-Violent Communication [300]

Co-Creator Radio Network [301]

Connections Radio [302]

---

[295] http://agnt.org/
[296] http://www.cosmicnature.net/cosmic_awakening.html
[297] http://awakening.net/Ezine.html
[298] http://bethechange.org.uk/
[299] http://www.forgiving.org/
[300] http://www.cnvc.org/
[301] http://co-creatornetwork.com/
[302] http://www.spiritmedianetwork.com/crs.htm

Conscious Living Radio [303]

Convergence Film [304]

Conversations with God for Kids [305]

David Wilcock: The Consciousness Field [306]

David Wilcock: The Source Field Investigations (SFI) Full Length Video [307]

Emerge and See: Waking Up In An Insane World [308]

Emissary of Light (James Twyman) [309]

---

303

http://www.podcastingnews.com/details/consciouslivingradio.org/mod
ules/blog/getrss.jsp/view.htm

304

http://divinecosmos.com/index.php?Itemid=34&id=17&option=com_c
ontent&sectionid=5&task=category

305 http://cwg4kids.com/

306 http://stevebeckow.com/2011/01/david-wilcock-consciousness-
field/

307 http://www.youtube.com/watch?v=nR-
klTa1y54&feature=player_embedded#!

308 http://emergeandsee.blogspot.com/

309 http://www.emissaryoflight.com/

EnlightenNext (Andrew Cohen) [310]

Fetzer Institute [311]

Foundation for Conscious Evolution [312]

Foundation for Pluralism [313]

Freewill, Fate and Causality in Matrix Reloaded [314]

Generation 21 [315]

Global Consciousness Project [316]

Global Mindshift [317]

Global Spirit [318]

---

[310] http://www.enlightennext.org/
[311] http://www.fetzer.org/
[312] http://barbaramarxhubbard.com/con/
[313] http://www.foundationforpluralism.com/
[314] http://montalk.net/metaphys/70/freewill-fate-and-causality-in-matrix-reloaded
[315] http://www.g21.com/
[316] http://noosphere.princeton.edu/
[317] http://www.global-mindshift.org/
[318] http://www.globalspirit.org/

How To Cultivate Compassion in Your Life [319]

Humanity's Team [320]

Institute for Sacred Activism (Andrew Harvey) [321]

Institute for Research on Unlimited Love [322]

Institute of Noetic Sciences [323]

Integral Institute [324]

International Association for Religious Freedom [325]

Kosmos [326]

Los Angeles Conscious Life Expo – 2012 Pineal Stargate Activation DVD (David Wilcock) [327]

---

[319] http://www.wikihow.com/Cultivate-Compassion-in-Your-Life
[320] http://www.humanitysteam.org/
[321] http://www.andrewharvey.net/
[322] http://www.unlimitedloveinstitute.org/
[323] http://www.noetic.org/
[324] http://www.integralinstitute.org/
[325] http://www.iarf.net/
[326] http://www.kosmosjournal.org/
[327] http://earthgrid.com/laexpo/dvd/david-wilcock-2011-dvd.html

Metanexus Institute [328]

Mind and Life Institute [329]

Mindfulness Journal [330]

Mindfulness Meditation Center [331]

New Spirituality Network [332]

Nonduality Salon (Jerry Katz) [333]

One Mind One Energy: The Power Is Within [334]

Oneness Minute [335]

Personal Authenticity Project [336]

---

[328] http://www.metanexus.net/
[329] http://www.mindandlife.org/
[330] http://www.springerlink.com/content/121591
[331] http://www.mindfulnessmeditationcentre.org/
[332] http://www.newspirituality.org/
[333] http://nonduality.com/
[334] http://www.one-mind-one-energy.com/
[335] http://www.onenessminute.org/
[336] http://personal-authenticity-project.com/markers-path-personal-authenticity

Phoenix Centre for Regenetics [337]

Principles of Spiritual Evolution (Part 1) [338]

Principles of Spiritual Evolution (Part 2) [339]

Principles of Spiritual Evolution (Part 3) [340]

Speed of Light Films [341]

Spiral Dynamics Integral [342]

Spiritual Media Network [343]

Stages of Conscious Awakening [344]

---

[337] http://www.phoenixregenetics.org/
[338] http://montalk.net/metaphys/42/principles-of-spiritual-evolution-part-i
[339] http://montalk.net/metaphys/43/principles-of-spiritual-evolution-part-ii
[340] http://montalk.net/metaphys/56/principles-of-spiritual-evolution-part-iii
[341] http://speedoflightfilms.com/
[342] http://www.spiraldynamics.net/
[343] http://www.spiritmedianetwork.com/index.htm
[344] http://montalk.net/metaphys/117/four-stages-of-conscious-awakening

Talking Dharma Project [345]

Teachings of Osho [346]

The Center for Compassion and Altruism and Education [347]

The Compassionate Instinct [348]

The Dalai Lama Foundation [349]

The Earth Charter Initiative [350]

The Forge Institute [351]

The Greater Good Science Center [352]

The Harmony Project [353]

---

[345] http://www.orderofcompassion.com/talkingdharma/author/admin/
[346] http://www.oshoteachings.com/
[347] http://ccare.stanford.edu/journal-articles
[348]

http://greatergood.berkeley.edu/article/item/the_compassionate_instinc
t/
[349] http://www.dalailamafoundation.org/dlf/en/index.jsp
[350] http://www.earthcharterinaction.org/content/
[351] http://www.theforge.org/site/content.php
[352] http://greatergood.berkeley.edu/
[353] http://www.theharmonyproject.org/index2.html

The Headless Way [354]

The Isha System [355]

The Network of Spiritual Progressives [356]

The Pineal Gland – The Bridge to Divine Consciousness [357]

The Spiritual Caucus at the United Nations [358]

The Values Caucus at the United Nations [359]

Transitions (Denise Le Fay) [360]

Truth and Reality [361]

Uniting People [362]

---

[354] http://www.headless.org/english-welcome.htm
[355] http://www.whywalkwhenyoucanfly.com/new/contenido.php?seccion=sistema_isha_intro
[356] http://spiritualprogressives.org/newsite/
[357] http://www.miraclesandinspiration.com/pinealgland.html
[358] http://www.spiritualcaucusun.org/
[359] http://www.valuescaucus.org/
[360] http://deniselefay.wordpress.com/
[361] http://www.spaceandmotion.com/
[362] http://www.unitingpeople.com/

Vision In Action [363]

Vivid Life [364]

ZenJoyMeditation [365]

## Disclosure

China's October Surprise (Part 1) [366]

China's October Surprise (Part 2) [367]

China's October Surprise (Part 3) [368]

China's October Surprise (Part 4) [369]

China's October Surprise (Part 5) [370]

---

[363] http://www.via-visioninaction.org/
[364] http://vividlife.me/ultimate/
[365] http://www.zenjoymeditation.com/
[366] http://divinecosmos.com/start-here/davids-blog/872-disclosureevent
[367] http://divinecosmos.com/start-here/davids-blog/896-chinasurprisequarantine
[368] http://divinecosmos.com/start-here/davids-blog/898-chinasurpriseiii
[369] http://divinecosmos.com/start-here/davids-blog/902-chinasurpriseradio
[370] http://divinecosmos.com/start-here/davids-blog/909-disclosurecriticalmass

China's October Surprise (Part 6) [371]

Disclosure Imminent [372]

Disclosure videos [373]

Divine Cosmos (David Wilcock) [374]

India Daily (excerpt one) [375]

India Daily (excerpt two) [376]

India Daily (excerpt three) [377]

India Daily (excerpt four) [378]

---

[371] http://www.divinecosmos.com/start-here/davids-blog/936-disclosurebinladen
[372] http://www.divinecosmos.com/start-here/davids-blog/975-undergroundbases
[373] http://www.divinecosmos.com/videos/free-videos-online/487-awesome-new-disclosure-videos
[374] http://www.divinecosmos.com/
[375] http://www.indiadaily.com/editorial/2656.asp
[376] http://www.indiadaily.com/editorial/20219.asp
[377] http://www.indiadaily.com/editorial/19513.asp
[378] http://www.indiadaily.com/editorial/10-09h-04.asp

India Daily (excerpt five) [379]

India Daily (excerpt six) [380]

India Daily (excerpt seven) [381]

India Daily (excerpt eight) [382]

India Daily (excerpt nine) [383]

India Daily (excerpt ten) [384]

India Daily (excerpt eleven) [385]

India Daily (excerpt twelve) [386]

India Daily (excerpt thirteen) [387]

---

[379] http://www.indiadaily.com/editorial/12-19c-04.asp
[380] http://www.indiadaily.com/editorial/01-23g-05.asp
[381] http://www.indiadaily.com/editorial/1651.asp
[382] http://www.indiadaily.com/editorial/1656.asp
[383] http://www.indiadaily.com/editorial/1801.asp
[384] http://www.indiadaily.com/editorial/2546.asp
[385] http://www.indiadaily.com/editorial/3835.asp
[386] http://www.indiadaily.com/editorial/7976.asp
[387] http://www.indiadaily.com/editorial/8306.asp

India Daily (excerpt fourteen) [388]

India Daily (excerpt fifteen) [389]

India Daily (excerpt sixteen) [390]

James Gilliland and ECETI [391]

SETI Institute [392]

The Disclosure Project [393]

The Importance of Disclosure [394]

**Education**

CosmiKids [395]

---

[388] http://www.indiadaily.com/editorial/14929.asp
[389] http://www.indiadaily.com/editorial/15022.asp
[390] http://www.indiadaily.com/editorial/15472.asp
[391] http://www.eceti.org/
[392] http://www.seti.org/
[393] http://www.disclosureproject.org/
[394] http://stevebeckow.com/wp-content/uploads/2011/07/The-Importance-of-Disclosure.pdf
[395] http://www.cosmikids.org/

One Spirit Learning Alliance [396]

Wisdom University [397]

**Empowerment**

Interview with Dr. Masaru Emoto [398]

Personal Development for Smart People [399]

The Orion Project [400]

**Esoteric Library**

Online Esoteric Library [401]

The Kybalion [402]

---

[396] http://www.onespiritinterfaith.org/
[397] https://www.wisdomuniversity.org/
[398] http://www.enwaterment.com/reiko-interview.html
[399] http://www.stevepavlina.com/index.htm
[400] http://www.theorionproject.org/en/index.html
[401] http://www.hermetics.org/ebooks.html
[402] http://gnostic.org/kybalionhtm/kybalion.htm

## Genetic Engineering of Food

GMO Dangers [403]

Hidden Danger's in Kids Meals [404]

Institute of Responsible Technology [405]

Non GMO Shopping Guide [406]

Non GMO Project [407]

Seeds of Deception [408]

Take Control of Your Health [409]

---

403

http://www.seedsofdeception.com/GMFree/GMODangers/index.cfm
[404] http://www.youtube.com/watch?v=hdHZl_U0764
[405] http://www.firstgiving.com/fundraiser/jeffrey-m-smith/instituteforresponsibletechnology
[406] http://www.nongmoshoppingguide.com/
[407] http://www.nongmoproject.org/industry/become-non-gmo-project-verified/
[408] http://www.seedsofdeception.com/Public/Home/index.cfm
409

http://search.mercola.com/search/pages/results.aspx?k=genetically%20modified%20foods

**Global Peace**

A Greenprint for Life [410]

Conflict Revolution [411]

Imagine Peace (Yoko Ono) [412]

Institute for Security and Cooperation in Outer Space [413]

Peace Council [414]

Temple of Understanding [415]

Think With Your Heart [416]

The Declaration of Human Freedom [417]

---

[410] http://www.greenprintforlife.org/
[411] http://www.barbarawith.com/
[412] http://imaginepeace.com/
[413] http://www.peaceinspace.com/treaty.htm
[414] http://www.peacecouncil.org/
[415] http://www.templeofunderstanding.org/
[416] http://www.thinkwithyourheart.net/
[417] http://stevebeckow.com/worldwide-march-millions/declaration-human-freedom/

The Free World Charter [418]

The Venus Project [419]

United Religions Initiative [420]

University for Peace [421]

**Health**

Dr. Mercola [422]

Dr. Valerie Hunt [423]

Energy Breakthrough [424]

EWG's Skin Deep Cosmetics Database [425]

---

[418] http://www.freeworldcharter.org/?a=charter
[419] http://www.thevenusproject.com/
[420] http://www.uri.org/
[421] http://www.upeace.org/
[422] http://www.mercola.com/
[423]
http://valerievhunt.com/ValerieVHunt.com/Valerie_Hunt_EdD.html
[424] http://stevebeckow.com/2011/05/media-ignores-energy-breakthrough-worry-free-nuclear-power/
[425] http://www.ewg.org/skindeep/

Global Soap Project [426]

Health Benefits of Listening to Music [427]

How Music Effects Us and Promotes Health [428]

Institute of HeartMath [429]

Music and the Brain [430]

**Inspirational**

Akiane Kramarik (art prodigy) [431]

Akiane Kramarik: Conversations [432]

Drawing Heaven (video about Akiane) [433]

---

[426] http://globalsoap.org/
[427] http://www.ibtimes.com/articles/139338/20110428/health-benefits-of-listening-to-music.htm
[428] http://www.emedexpert.com/tips/music.shtml
[429] http://www.heartmath.org/
[430] http://www.cerebromente.org.br/n15/mente/musica.html
[431] http://www.artakiane.com/home
[432] http://www.youtube.com/watch?v=cYDzUTZys8g&NR=1
[433] http://www.youtube.com/watch?v=rmm-0-Rdxo8

OM Times Magazine [434]

Society for Universal Sacred Music [435]

**The Law of One**

Ra Material: Law of One [436]

The Law of One [437]

**Social Conditioning**

101 Negative Money Beliefs [438]

Anger Management [439]

Battle of Opposites [440]

Opening the Flow [441].

---

[434] http://omtimes.com/
[435] http://www.universalsacredmusic.org/
[436] http://www.spiritofra.com/Ra-section%201.htm
[437] http://www.lawofone.info/
[438] http://www.abundancetapestry.com/101-negative-money-beliefs/
[439] http://www.angermanagementtips.com/exercises.htm
[440] http://montalk.net/metaphys/97/battle-of-opposites
[441] http://montalk.net/metaphys/88/opening-the-flow

Remove Social Conditioning and Return to Natural Enlightenment [442]

Transforming Your Beliefs About Money [443]

**Truth**

2012 Indy Info [444]

Divine Cosmos YouTube Channel [445]

Julian Assange [446]

Mellen-Thomas Benedict [447]

Michael Parenti [448]

---

[442] http://channelhigherself.com/videos/satsang-with-the-self/remove-social-conditioning-return-to-natural-enlightenment/
[443] http://www.taoofprosperity.com/transforming-your-beliefs-about-money/
[444] http://2012indyinfo.wordpress.com/
[445] http://www.youtube.com/davidwilcock333
[446] http://www.huffingtonpost.com/news/julian-assange/
[447] http://www.mellen-thomas.com/home.htm
[448] http://www.michaelparenti.org/index.html

My Own Revolution [449]

Neil Kramer [450]

OpenLeaks [451]

Open Your Mind Ireland radio show [452]

The 2012 Scenario (activist Steve Beckow) [453]

The Cosmic Laws of Awareness [454]

The Essays of Brother Anonymous [455]

True Reality Creation (Part 1) [456]

True Reality Creation (Part 2) [457]

---

[449] http://www.myownrevolution.net/
[450] http://neilkramer.com/
[451] http://www.openleaks.org/
[452] http://www.oymireland.com/
[453] http://stevebeckow.com/
[454] http://www.cosmicchannelings.com/blog/universal-laws
[455] http://www.angelfire.com/space2/light11/index.html
[456] http://montalk.net/metaphys/68/true-reality-creation-part-i
[457] http://montalk.net/metaphys/69/true-reality-creation-part-ii

Truth Contest [458]

WikiLeaks (Julian Assange) [459]

Wisdom à la carte [460]

---

[458] http://www.truthcontest.com/
[459] http://wikileaks.org/
[460] http://wisdomalacarte.net/blog/

Michele Doucette is webmistress of Portals of Spirit, a spirituality website whereby one will find links to [1] The Enlightened Scribe, [2] an ezine called Gateway To The Soul, [3] books of spiritual resonance as well as authors of metaphysical importance, [4] categories of interest from Angels to Zen, [5] up-to-date information as shared by a Quantum Healer, [6] affiliate programs and resources of personal significance, [7] healing resource advertisements and [8] spiritual news.

As a Level 2 Reiki Practitioner, she sends long distance Reiki to those who make the request, claiming only to be a facilitator of the Universal energy, meaning that it is up to the individual(s) in question to use these energies in order to heal themselves.

Having also acquired a Crystal Healing Practitioner diploma (Stonebridge College in the UK), she is guardian to many from the mineral kingdom.

She is the author of several spiritual/metaphysical works; namely, [1] *The Ultimate Enlightenment For 2012: All We Need Is Ourselves*, a book that was nominated for the Allbooks Review Best Inspirational Book for 2011, [2] *Turn Off The TV: Turn On Your Mind*, [3] *Veracity At Its Best*, [4] *The Collective: Essays on Reality* (a composition of essays in relation to the Matrix), [5] *Sleepers Awaken: The Time Is Now To Consciously Create Your Own Reality*, [6] *Healing the Planet and Ourselves: How To Raise Your Vibration*, [7] *You Are Everything: Everything Is You*, [8] *The Awakening of Humanity: A Foremost Necessity*, and [9] *The Cosmos of the Soul: A Spiritual Biography*, all of which have been published through St. Clair Publications.

In addition, she has written a separate volume that deals with crystals, aptly entitled *The Wisdom of Crystals*.

She is also the author of *A Travel in Time to Grand Pré*, a visionary metaphysical novel that historically ties the descendants of Yeshua (Jesus) to modern day Nova Scotia.

As shared by a reviewer, it is *Veracity At Its Best*, a spiritual (metaphysical) tome, that "constructs the context for the spiritual message" imparted in *A Travel in Time to Grand Pré*.

Against the backdrop of 1754 Acadie, it was the blending of French Acadian history with current DNA testing that contributed to the weaving of this alchemical tale of time travel, romance and intrigue.

From Henry I Sinclair to the Merovingians, from the Cathari treasure at Montségur to the Knights Templar, this novel, together with the words of Yeshua as spoken at the height of his ministry, has the potential to inspire others; for it is herein that we learn how individuals can find their way, their truth(s), so as to live their lives to the fullest.

She is currently working on *Back Home with Evangeline*, the sequel to *A Travel in Time to Grand Pré*.

10408726R00164

Made in the USA
Charleston, SC
02 December 2011